GROUNDED LITERACIES IN A TRANSNATIONAL WAC/WID ECOLOGY: A KOREAN-U.S. STUDY

INTERNATIONAL EXCHANGES ON THE STUDY OF WRITING

Series Editors: Joan Mullin, Magnus Gustafsson, Terry Myers Zawacki, and Federico Navarro

Series Associate Editors: Anna S. Habib and Karen P. Peirce

The International Exchanges on the Study of Writing Series publishes books that address worldwide perspectives on writing, writers, teaching with writing, and scholarly writing practices, specifically those that draw on scholarship across national and disciplinary borders to challenge parochial understandings of all of the above. The Latin America Section of the International Exchanges on the Study of Writing book series publishes peer-reviewed books about writing, writers, teaching with writing, and scholarly writing practices from Latin American perspectives. It also offers re-editions of recognized peer-reviewed books originally published in the region.

The WAC Clearinghouse and University Press of Colorado are collaborating so that these books will be widely available through free digital distribution and low-cost print editions. The publishers and the series editors are committed to the principle that knowledge should freely circulate and have embraced the use of technology to support open access to scholarly work.

RECENT BOOKS IN THE SERIES

Magnus Gustafsson and Andreas Eriksson (Eds.), *Negotiating the Intersections of Writing and Writing Instruction* (2022)

L. Ashley Squires (Ed.), *Emerging Writing Research from the Russian Federation* (2021)

Natalia Ávila Reyes (Ed.), *Multilingual Contributions to Writing Research: Toward an Equal Academic Exchange* (2021)

Cecile Badenhorst, Brittany Amell, and James Burford (Eds.), *Re-imagining Doctoral Writing* (2021)

Bruce Morrison, Julia Chen, Linda Lin, and Alan Urmston (Eds.), *English Across the Curriculum: Voices from Around the World* (2021)

Alanna Frost, Julia Kiernan, and Suzanne Blum Malley (Eds.), *Translingual Dispositions: Globalized Approaches to the Teaching of Writing* (2020)

Charles Bazerman et al. (Eds.), *Knowing Writing: Writing Research across Borders* (2019)

Sylvie Plane et al. (Eds.), *Research on Writing: Multiple Perspectives* (2017)

Lisa R. Arnold, Anne Nebel, and Lynne Ronesi (Eds.), *Emerging Writing Research from the Middle East-North Africa Region* (2017)

GROUNDED LITERACIES IN A TRANSNATIONAL WAC/WID ECOLOGY: A KOREAN-U.S. STUDY

By Jay Jordan

The WAC Clearinghouse
wac.colostate.edu
Fort Collins, Colorado

University Press of Colorado
upcolorado.com
Denver, Colorado

The WAC Clearinghouse, Fort Collins, Colorado 80523

University Press of Colorado, Denver, Colorado 80202

ISBN 978-1-64215-150-3 (PDF) | 978-1-64215-151-0 (ePub) | 978-1-64642-346-0 (pbk.)

DOI 10.37514/INT-B.2022.1503

Produced in the United States of America

Library of Congress Cataloging-in-Publication Data

Names: Jordan, Jay, 1973– author.
Title: Grounded literacies in a transnational WAC/WID ecology : a Korean-U.S. study / by Jay Jordan.
Description: Fort Collins, Colorado : The WAC Clearinghouse ; Louisville, Colorado : University Press of Colorado, [2022] | Series: International exchanges on the study of writing | Includes bibliographical references.
Identifiers: LCCN 2022018560 (print) | LCCN 2022018561 (ebook) | ISBN 9781646423460 (paperback) | ISBN 9781642151503 (adobe pdf) | ISBN 9781642151510 (epub)
Subjects: LCSH: University of Utah. Asia Campus—Administration. | English language—Rhetoric—Study and teaching (Higher)—Korea (South) | English language—Study and teaching (Higher)—Social aspects—Korea (South) | English language—Social aspects—Korea (South) | Transnational education—Korea (South) | Interdisciplinary approach in education—Korea (South)
Classification: LCC PE1068.K6 J67 2022 (print) | LCC PE1068.K6 (ebook) | DDC 428.0071/05195—dc23/eng/20220615
LC record available at https://lccn.loc.gov/2022018560
LC ebook record available at https://lccn.loc.gov/2022018561

Copyeditor: Meg Vezzu
Design and Production: Mike Palmquist
Cover Photo: University of Utah
Series Editors: Joan Mullin, Magnus Gustafsson, Terry Myers Zawacki, and Federico Navarro
Series Associate Editors: Anna S. Habib and Karen P. Peirce

The WAC Clearinghouse supports teachers of writing across the disciplines. Hosted by Colorado State University, it brings together scholarly journals and book series as well as resources for teachers who use writing in their courses. This book is available in digital formats for free download at wac.colostate.edu.

Founded in 1965, the University Press of Colorado is a nonprofit cooperative publishing enterprise supported, in part, by Adams State University, Colorado State University, Fort Lewis College, Metropolitan State University of Denver, University of Alaska Fairbanks, University of Colorado, University of Denver, University of Northern Colorado, University of Wyoming, Utah State University, and Western Colorado University. For more information, visit upcolorado.com.

Land Acknowledgment. The Colorado State University Land Acknowledgment can be found at https://landacknowledgment.colostate.edu.

Contents

§ Preface

Writing this preface now more than six years after my return from a year-long appointment at the University of Utah Asia Campus (UAC)—a place I describe in this book—I am unavoidably conscious that much of what I detail here would currently be impossible. Pandemic-related travel restrictions remain in place in 2022 and probably will continue to limit travel for the foreseeable future. With a much smaller percentage of COVID-19 infection than my native United States has, South Korea (henceforth Korea) nonetheless continues to be extremely vigilant about entry of foreigners—not to mention internal movements of its own citizens and residents.

However, I am privileged to remain engaged with the Asia Campus, albeit from nearly 6,000 miles and—depending on Daylight Savings Time—15 to 16 hours away. I have served as a member of the extended campus' executive committee, which oversees budgetary decisions, the additions of new academic majors, the appointment of new campus administrators, and efforts to coordinate and collaborate with the several other universities also operating foreign campuses in New Songdo City. I have been on several other committees recruiting and hiring new faculty members for writing courses there. I have worked with graduate and undergraduate students interested in researching international education for whom the Asia Campus is an intriguing and accessible site. And I have most recently co-taught an online course on English as an international language in which a colleague and I have combined her Asia Campus students with my US-based campus students at the very narrow sweet spot on the clock when we can meet synchronously. We hope this course is only the first of others that help our students connect across distance—especially at a time when a global pandemic makes the distance seem especially long.

Neither this book nor these other opportunities would have been possible without the generous, consistent, creative support of many faculty colleagues, administrators, staff members, and students—a number of whom appear pseudonymously in chapters that follow. I can and will name Robert Newman, former dean of the University of Utah College of Humanities and current president and director of the National Humanities Center, who asked me to go to the brand-new Asia Campus in the first place. My friend, colleague, and former program director and chair, Maureen Mathison, graciously and willingly assented to my going even though it left our then-tiny fledgling department short-staffed, and even though it delayed my return to the

US as incoming department chair. As the Asia Campus' first chief academic officer, Stephen Walston adeptly led colleagues and me into the unknown large and small considerations of administering and teaching at a brand-new site, setting a vision and helping unpack and distribute textbooks—often simultaneously. Successive chief global officers Michael Hardman and Chris Ireland kept us connected to the broader university from its home base and laid groundwork for Asia Campus students' transitions to the US for at least a year of study, and they spoke with me about their direct involvement in the campus' founding vision. They also contributed funding for travel, accommodations, and food for research assistants and me on trips to Korea in 2016, 2017, and 2018.

I cannot write glowingly enough about those research assistants—all academics and/or professionals in their own right. Charissa Che applied her sharply critical eye and resulting insights about the ways "Asian" student identities circulate in higher education. Joanne Castillo contributed boundless curiosity, asking questions I had not thought to ask. Justin Grant Whitney traveled with prior experience in and love for Korea, which helped me and the Asia Campus faculty members he met there understand the context just a bit more. All three were invaluable collaborators in interviews and observations about classroom activities and the Asia Campus more broadly. Indeed, the impressions and insights they shared on our trips connected that campus' pedagogical work even more closely with its natural and built environments as those environments were constantly evolving.

All writers can tend to be a little too close to what they are writing and thus unable to imagine other arrangements, ideas, and possibilities. My academic and personal commitments to this book have inspired my writing but, at times, have run the risk of propelling me too quickly past important details that make this transnational educational experiment richly complex. So I am extremely fortunate that Terry Myers Zawacki is such an able and sensitive reader. I am further deeply grateful to Terry's enthusiastically supportive editorial colleagues, Magnus Gustafsson, Anna Sophia Habib, and Joan Mullin, and to the two anonymous reviewers whose incisive comments made this manuscript far better.

Last, I thank the people who have shared my space even while I, many times, have lived far more inside my head than truly in their presence. Davis Jordan and Jennifer Neal love me unconditionally, and it shows. I was away from them for almost a full year at the start of this project, and I have found reasons to travel here and there since I came back. But even if they do not always go with me, they are always the best part of me.

GROUNDED LITERACIES IN A TRANSNATIONAL WAC/WID ECOLOGY: A KOREAN-U.S. STUDY

Introduction. Orienting to a Startup within a Startup within a Startup

I taught at my university's first-ever foreign campus, located in New Songdo City, Korea, during its first academic year of operation, 2014-15. Not only was our campus new, but the entire city around it was as well. My colleagues and I became sharp observers of how a then 100,000-person urban experiment built in part to meet international demands *on spec* would function under pressure of *actual* international consumer demands. Over the course of 11 months, I watched both small mom-and-pop stores and local outlets of Korean big box conglomerates shift inventories to carry more cereal, muesli, peanut butter, and Belgian beer. I also saw significant changes in coffee. While Korea's coffee culture had been growing steadily since U.S.-based popular culture became a fixture after the early 1950s war, it expanded rapidly after Korea's economic recovery in the late 1990s. Both in our city and on numerous visits to Korea's massive capital, Seoul, I typically encountered coffee houses whose baristas would look at me quizzically when I ordered something *other* than a cute, sweetened, pre-measured espresso beverage. But then in seemingly no time, Korea adapted U.S.- and Japan-based artisanal coffee engineering and rapidly distributed it countrywide. By 2016—only a year after I had left—Seoul had more than 17,000 coffee retail stores. That was more per capita than either San Francisco or Seattle (Lee & Kim, 2016).

But Korea's embrace of retail coffee culture is not merely an example of straightforward importation. Granted, the very American brand, Starbucks, was the thin end of the wedge at the front of this trend, opening its first store in Seoul in 1999 (Lee & Kim, 2016). However, another Seoul Starbucks outlet's sign is likely recognizable even to those who *cannot* read its native Korean-language (*hangeul*) characters: the transliteration for "Starbucks Coffee" (스타벅스커피) stands out prominently on a touristy street in Seoul's popular Insadong neighborhood. Less recognizable perhaps is the juxtaposition of those characters alongside the more common English-language Starbucks marketing that nearly universally circulates everywhere *else* in Seoul and beyond—and the puzzling appearance of this clear assertion of Korean language in the middle of an overtly international area. While I have not yet tracked down an authoritative rationale behind this sign, I *have* become quite familiar with some of the complexities of Korea's location in a globalized

3

economy in which English is a putatively stable, acquirable, and tradable commodity. My year in Korea taught me about the country's pride in its language, its food, its long national history, its baseball, its ambitious megastructural building projects, its investment in advanced technologies, and its desire to project Korean culture abroad. It also taught me about its insular management cultures, its intense and anxiety-ridden education system, its negative if not poisonous relationship with Japan, and its simultaneous fascination with and hesitations about the United States.

On our campus in New Songdo City, colleagues and I quickly became aware that we were part of a large and visible investment in Korean-American relations—one with stakeholders at the home campus of my university; among the administrators of the "Asia Campus"; in the offices of the educational foundation behind the campus, the local free enterprise zone authority, various private-public partners literally building the city around us, and the education ministry; and at the U.S. Embassy in Seoul. Along with several other colleagues as well as administrators and students, I appeared during brief news interviews on an English-language Korean television network to answer questions about what the campus was and why it was there. And Korean/Korean-speaking staff members regularly updated us on stories about the campus in local and national print/online media outlets. Meanwhile, we were beginning to teach, advise, support, coordinate, and plan under the authority and with the brand of a major U.S.-based university.

I joked with colleagues and friends then and I have since that I had just finished reading Kim Stanley Robinson's Mars trilogy (*Red Mars*, *Green Mars*, and *Blue Mars*), in which an initially small but diverse cast of explorers begins colonizing and terraforming a new planet. Mars' first human residents needed to build habitats with the materials they brought with them, repurposing spacecraft shipping containers as housing. We were far more privileged at the Asia Campus, moving into recently built apartments a short walk from classroom, office, and administrative spaces. But the "explorers" metaphor stuck as we walked or cycled to the center of "town" or to metro stations a kilometer or more away to shop for groceries. It continued to stick the more we learned about the ecological impacts of "reclaiming" land from the Yellow Sea.

To the confusion and maybe annoyance of a couple of editors who have read earlier/shorter drafts or installments of this book, the tendency I just displayed above to drift between intellectual/conceptual context and a detailed description of actual, daily life at the Asia Campus feels unavoidable. I was perhaps primed to pay specific kinds of attention to the campus not only by my science fiction reading but also by the emergence of my interest in affect and vital materialism, evident in an article I was drafting about my preoccupation with the intersection of materialist thinking, rhetoric, and translingual composition, which I was revising as I transitioned to Korea (Jordan, 2015). As part of that project, I read across several fields, including posthumanist and speculative philosophy, and I was prompted to think about the "context" of my situation by casting as wide a net as possible. Of course, my background in second language writing and rhetoric and composition had already predisposed me to think about language work in social terms, but it had been nearly 20 years since I myself had felt especially sensitive about my own social and material surrounds while living and working. As a Peace Corps volunteer in Poland in the late 1990s, I could not leave my apartment without encountering ubiquitous symbols and sensory inputs reminding me I was far from home. To this day, I have sensitive ears for Polish (even if I don't quite understand the individual words) and a sensitive nose for dill, perfectly ripe strawberries, and the burning coal that meant cooking and heating in many parts of that country. Those intellectual, social, and sensory experiences are inextricable from one another, and the unique environs of the Asia Campus acted on me similarly. While the impetus for this project was scholarly—born from an urge to learn from my university's great international experiment that was part of an even larger international experiment—I have been unable to pursue it without daily encountering a complex set of memories and impressions. Recalling the courses I taught, the students I met, and the writing I did also recalls/re-embodies the colleagues who became close friends; the smells of red pepper paste and of dust blowing onshore from as far away as the Gobi Desert; the sounds of massive trucks hauling dredged earth for the city-scale construction project in which we lived and of consistently polite Korean recordings on the metro trains announcing next stops; and the tastes of street food, of gracious home cooking, and of impromptu meetings in, of all places, the Mexican restaurant underneath the Irish pub.

There I go again. But I was not alone. As the participants in this project relate in explicit and implicit ways, whether they were living, learning, and working in their formally defined "home" country or not, some part of this experience was novel for each of them. Mostly monolingual native English speakers, myself included, were working at an English-medium institution created and self-consciously styled as an "extended" campus and not a "branch" campus of our U.S.-based university, but we were in meaningful ways answerable to Korean authorities who had never set foot on the U.S.-based home campus, who spoke Korean exclusively, and who were oriented to management methods that seemed opaque to many of my colleagues and me.[1] Students, the vast majority of whom were Korean nationals, were in a familiar country but also subject to the expectations of a university very different from the domestic institutions many of their peers were attending—including at least three such institutions that were a brief walk from our campus. And all of us were living in a city that was rising out of the sea around us, shaping us and being shaped. That city in turn was part of a very old but simultaneously very young and dynamic country investing heavily in higher education and eager to find ways forward with an equally eager U.S.-based partner university.

Goals and Questions

This study represents a major investment in understanding that aspirational educational experiment through my experiences as a scholar-teacher working alongside students and colleagues—all of us affecting and affected by an emerging transnational scene.

I have remained engaged with the Asia Campus in ways that perhaps continue to blur lines between advocacy for and scholarship about international education. I have traveled back to the Asia Campus several times with funding from university offices with vested interests in the campus' success. I have been fascinated on each visit to discover ways the campus and city have changed—often drastically in the form of entire new buildings and even newly reclaimed land. I have served on the executive committee that helps oversee administrative decisions on the campus. I have promoted the campus to prospective new faculty hires in my home department. And, all along, I have read literature on international and transnational[2] education—and on international branch campuses, specifically; on English's spread and evolution in Korea; on writing in the majors/disciplines represented on the Asia Campus; and on the transfer of knowledge about and practices of writing.

Focusing on students' writing made sense, of course, because of my background and interests, which include a legacy of scholarship that assumes or

---

1 According to my university's former chief global officer, Michael Hardman (personal communication, October 22, 2020), the university had described and begun marketing the Asia Campus as an "extended" rather than a "branch" campus in order to emphasize for Korean government authorities, students, and families the curricular equivalence between campuses. But the university formalized that description when the U.S. Department of Education notified it that it needed to ensure that the Asia Campus' operations complied with applicable U.S. laws. Once it had ensured compliance, university students could then use federally guaranteed financial aid to pay tuition at either campus.

2 A distinction I discuss in detail in Chapter 1.

argues explicitly for the value of writing in higher education. My focus also made sense because Asia Campus administrators in connection with colleagues in my home department decided to depart from historical practice by requiring all Asia Campus students to take both of the required lower-division writing courses at the university instead of allowing some students to place out of one of the courses based on high school grade point average and standardized test scores. (Thus, one of the new campus' innovations was literally doubling down on the university's emphasis on writing education.) More broadly, my focus seemed highly relevant to ongoing efforts in the field to understand what students can learn about writing in one context and then transfer to another—a new course, new discipline, or new location—especially as those efforts continue in many institutions that are actively seeking more diverse students and more global connections.

But as I will relate in detail in Chapter 4, there are serious and complex questions about the extent to which what students know about and do with writing actually transfers from one course or from another context to the next. Some scholars go as far as questioning the value of teaching writing altogether: Ilona Leki (2007) concludes her longitudinal study of four multilingual undergraduate students on a note of pessimism about whether any writing class can teach most of what students need to know to write effectively (p. 284). But behind that claim is Leki's clear statement that writing is not irrelevant—just that it must be studied as one activity among many others, not set in sole relief against a static contextual backdrop. She writes,

> what has been enhanced for me is my sense of the importance
> of attempting to understand not just the individuals seated in
> a given classroom but also how those individuals negotiate the
> complexities of the social, cultural, academic, and sociopoliti-
> cal environments that surround them. (Leki, 2007, p. 285)

Leki's realization promises to be humbling for both teachers and researchers. As both a teacher and researcher myself, I have been humbled as I have been steeped in such scholarly realizations and related advice. I was certainly humbled on arriving at the Asia Campus, situated as it is at the nexus of overlapping "social, cultural, academic, and sociopolitical environments"—a nexus at which students, colleagues, and I were enacting on a daily basis and at many scales the broad vision that was intended to guide this new campus.

In short, I have wanted since early in my time at the Asia Campus to ask questions similar to those Leki (2007) and other scholars I survey in this book have asked about what "context" really means beyond the scope of an assignment or course. Such questions, of course, are not new to second language writing, composition studies, or Writing Across the Curriculum/Writing in Disciplines (WAC/WID). But the experiment in which I found myself definitely made "context" more sensible and more immediate than it had been in my previous experiences.

My goal thus became to study what happens to writing across the curriculum and in disciplines as a highly privileged activity within an especially dynamic "context"—an aspirational university's brand-new campus located in an aspirational new city in an aspirational country. Indeed, a startup within a startup within a startup with all the futuristic optimism and messy uncertainty that description suggests. And since international education efforts are only becoming more complex due to changes in immigration policies, the proliferation of digital communication platforms, varying country-level restrictions on those platforms, and most recently a global pandemic, it seems that paying even closer attention to the roles writing education can and does play in experiments like my own university's makes sense.

As one of the first faculty members to travel to the new campus in 2014, I was asked to teach a first-year seminar course and to provide writing center-style tutorial assistance to the first student cohorts. I offered to provide WAC/WID support for faculty colleagues as well based on the understanding that I was as interested in supporting colleagues' creation of effective writing assignments as I was in helping students—an interest that had arisen during a study of faculty attitudes about writing instruction in engineering, in which my collaborator and I learned both how much writing was a preoccupation among faculty and how little faculty colleagues shared their knowledge about writing (see Jordan & Kedrowicz, 2011). In the Asia Campus' compact and cohesive setting, I saw an opportunity to study writing and interactions around writing more closely. Specifically, I saw an opportunity to go beyond the surface-level claims about internationalization that Tiane Donahue (2009) critiques—claims predicated on what she terms an "import/export" (p. 212) model of knowledge-making that fails to cultivate "deep familiarity" (p. 236) with contexts outside the US. Given that Asia Campus students were also required to spend at least a year of their academic careers at the U.S.-based campus, I also saw an opportunity to study the effects of that kind of transition. So, primed by my own previous research on WAC/WID and second language writing as well as other published scholarship, and aware of the university's emphasis on the primacy of writing in the new campus' curricula, I generated an initial set of writing- and pedagogy-focused research questions:

- How is writing being explicitly and implicitly taught in courses across the curriculum at the new campus?

- What kinds of writing are instructors assigning across the curriculum?
- How do students perceive/respond to the writing assignments and teaching?
- How do instructors respond to the students' writing?
- What effects do students' transitions from the international campus to the U.S. campus have on their own and their instructors' perceptions and responses?

While those questions consistently guided interviews and my analyses of other data about writing, I understood from the beginning of my study, as I have noted, that the complexity of that writing's "context" made it impossible for me to isolate writing from its surrounds. Thus, I added this question to my initial list:

- How does writing as a privileged literate activity reveal the relationship between internationalist claims about education and the daily, lived complexity behind such claims?

This book thus draws from WAC/WID as well as several related fields, including second language writing and rhetoric and composition, to describe through participants' and my own meaning making the ways writing has figured as a key collection of knowledges and practices that help shape and are shaped by this university's complexity. Despite what I will relate later as the smoothly marketable promise of such an educational experiment, the campus', the university's, the host city's, and Korea's mutual embeddedness exemplifies, reinforces, and provides nuance to scholarly arguments that literacies—in this case, literacies developing in conditions of daily cultural and language contact—may certainly be supported by classroom and curricular plans for teaching and learning but can never be reducible to them.

Chapter Outline

Chapter 1 provides an overview of "international" and "transnational" perspectives on education as those terms relate to and diverge from each other to provide context for my study. Chapter 1 also discusses Korea's complex relationship with English and with English-language education as that country has aspired to a more international stature—a stature that attracted my university's establishment of a campus and that continues to inform its presence there. Given the inextricability of my daily lived experience as a resident of the startup campus and startup city from my study itself, Chapter 2 provides a critical narrative of that experience and its connections with the scholarly, pedagogical, and administrative work with which I was engaged. Chapter 3 more fully introduces and describes my research site as well as the methodological considerations guiding my study.

In the context of existing scholarship in WID and also in teaching communication and psychology (the fields in which student-participants were majoring), Chapter 4 contends that students in my study do not simply carry writing knowledge with them from course to course and campus to campus but instead repurpose and reorient to knowledge and experiences, testing their utility at the nexus of personal interests/backgrounds and academic requirements. The chapter also observes that faculty members in my study, while insistent on rigorous introductions to their disciplines, are similarly sensitive to the disciplines' sociality and to their own ongoing socialization to the transnational context.

In Chapter 5, I focus on one student's motivation to naturalize her own language competency as she builds personal and professional identities. Some second language writers' identity work has been described in terms that foreground their coping with intransigent academic and professional demands; however, students like this one act in ways beyond "coping," skillfully and even ambitiously identifying affordances in an ecological push and pull with teachers and mentors. At the same time, far from representing static targets for academic competence, faculty members are often aware of and responsive to students' varied goals. And even when they are not aware, their interactions with and reflections about students demonstrate that learning in this transnational context is more than the sum of its explicit parts. It is indeed natural and, thus, considerably more complex than the explicit setup of courses and curricula.

Chapter 6 views English's complexity in Korea through the work and reflections of another student. While English competence is a mark of status and achievement in Korea, "competence" can be a moving target as a result of the country's evolving international relations and related language politics. For the focal student in this chapter in particular, the match between his familial/phenotypical Koreanness and his cultural and linguistic Americanness is uncertain, and that uncertainty affects his relationships with peers and faculty members. More broadly, it represents ambiguity about the relationship between fixed language standards and language's actual spread.

In Chapter 7, I conclude by reflecting on teaching, learning, observing, and experiencing in this transnational experiment, arguing that the ongoing evolution of transnational education necessitates empirical sensitivity as well as a keen awareness that relevant writing-related scholarship, teaching, and administration are inextricable from one another.

1 Orienting to Transnational English-Language Education in Korea

The relevance to this book of cross-border education, the spread of English as an international language, and Korea's relatively recent openness to international contact necessitate a discussion about how those topics influence my own perspective before entering my research site. So in this chapter, I provide background on several conceptual frameworks that sensitized me and guided my travel and work between my U.S.-based and Korea-based campuses. In describing these frameworks, I also suggest the necessity of similar conceptual grounding for other, similar work regardless of national contexts.

International/Transnational Education

Both the terms "international" and "transnational" appear in my study—in part because both terms circulate in relevant literature and in my university's description of its own work at both its campuses. But the two terms are not ultimately interchangeable.

Internationalization and Branch Campuses

"Internationalization" as a buzzword in U.S.-based higher education typically refers to efforts to engage with other national contexts. Those efforts include recruiting international students, creating and sustaining learning abroad opportunities for domestic students, building small- or large-scale branch campuses of U.S. universities (as my university did), identifying foreign sites for research and technology development, and partnering with foreign educational institutions to promote awareness of specific universities as brands in globalizing markets.

A lot of what is known about international students in the US is captured superficially but compellingly by the numbers. The Institute of International Education's (2022) annual *Open Doors* report observes that roughly 1.1 million students (including over 52,000 Koreans) came to the US to study in tertiary institutions during the 2018–19 academic year, a figure that represents the 12th year in a row of growth or steadiness despite recent perceived and actual shifts in U.S. policies and attitudes that have been unfavorable for international student recruitment.[3]

My own university/research site is an example of another international trend. Adding to students' traditional patterns of travel from home to host country, a phenomenon that Anna Kosmützky has termed a "California gold rush" of international branch campuses (IBCs) has established new U.S.-based college and university sites in countries ranging from Albania to Qatar to Rwanda (as cited in Redden, 2015). The Cross-Border Education Research Team (C-BERT), a multi-institution and multidisciplinary collective, defines such campuses as entities owned by foreign education providers that offer degrees "substantially on site" in those foreign providers' names in host countries (C-BERT, n.d.). As of late 2020, C-BERT lists roughly 300 international campuses coordinated by 37 countries (up from 180 campuses in the last decade), among which the United States is the largest exporter. My university's Asia Campus is in good company—part of what Jason Lane and Kevin Kinser (2013) describe as an "Asia Pivot" among universities based in the US, UK, and Australia through which Western-style institutions can locate at least some programs closer to extremely large markets for students in Korea, China, Malaysia, and other rapidly developing countries in the region.

IBCs often launch on the assumption that they can export desirable curricula to students who demand U.S.-style university education but wish to remain close to home. Universities following the trend tend to propagate what Stephen Wilkins and Jeroen Huisman (2012) term "isomorphic" educational and administrative models and practices across borders, especially where the governments that invite them are interested in promoting new efforts based on those universities' identities and reputations: for instance, it was clear early on in my university's negotiations with Korea's Ministry of Education that we were expected to offer the same degree programs with the same transcripts as the U.S.-based campus. But such high-level negotiations between university administrators and host country education officials may lead to provisional agreements that lack faculty support (or even knowledge).

---

3   As I revise this chapter, COVID-19, the infectious syndrome caused by the novel coronavirus SARS-CoV-2, continues to spread and kill. Immediate and long-term effects on international students' entry to the United States remain uncertain, and the pandemic has definitely impacted enrollment in the short term. But universities such as my own are attempting to extend synchronous and asynchronous online instruction to other countries in attempts to maintain international student engagement. For our extended campus, the pandemic has meant that some students who would have shifted their studies to the US have remained in place and are attempting to enroll in online courses to augment the courses that remain for them there.

Initial challenges may also include funding and policy. Funding models typically rely on money approved by local governments or foundations with widely different ideas about budgetary transparency. University standards of academic freedom may clash with restraints on speech in destinations such as China, Singapore, and the United Arab Emirates (Redden, 2014; 2019). As Wilkins and Huisman (2012) note, the values that undergird high levels of parental investment in education in countries such as China and Korea can also inform those countries' tight educational controls—controls that may seem obscure, obstructionist, or even xenophobic to educational entities coming from other countries.

In addition to the challenges that emerge at high levels of planning and implementation, clear mismatches can arise at more daily operational levels too. Peter Ninnes and Meeri Hellstén (2005) argue that "the internationalization of higher education is currently experiencing a moment of exhaustion brought on by increasing workload demands and seemingly insoluble pedagogical dilemmas" (pp. 3–4). And even where U.S.-based universities successfully navigate their entry, the large investments in student affairs at their "home" campuses may not translate to international branches, where a lack of country-specific experience with counseling, housing/residence life, and other wraparound services may cause problems for students, especially if they transition from one campus to the other (Cicchetti, 2018; Ludeman et al., 2009). Employees themselves may also face challenges owing to the interactions of different professional cultures and expectations: in a study of staffing at six IBCs, Farshid Shams and Jeroen Huisman (2016) conclude that institutions' need to balance hiring from "home" and "local" contexts can lead to disparate employment terms and treatment. Li Cai and Christine Hall (2016) point to the need for sustained and targeted professional development to help faculty members anticipate and adjust to the many potential differences between home and local *academic* contexts in addition to immediate *personal* and *social* needs.

A Transnational Approach

In most cases, as in the case of the Korea-based campus that is a large part of my own research site, international priorities at high administrative and policymaking levels give way to many complexities where students, faculty, staff, and other community members within and adjacent to institutional sites actually work and live. Theorists of "transnationalism" apply analytic and often critical lenses to such complexities to claim that what appear to be people's discretely separate national identities are actually "constructed within and often solidified by transnational connections" (Hesford & Schell, 2008, p. 464; also see Martins, 2015). As Thomas Faist et al. (2013) argue, the phenomenon of migration, for instance, may appear to move people from one place to another, but it actually creates "transnational social space," which transcends specific circumstances of geography to create imagined/virtual sensibilities in which a migrant identifies with multiple places simultaneously through "repeated movements and, above all, continued transactions" (p. 1; see also Levitt & Schiller, 2004). Steven Vertovec (1999) argues that transnationalism may mean a kind of consciousness, but it also describes patterns of capital flow, sites for political engagement, and "social morphologies" exemplified by split families whose members live in and feel allegiance to several countries, often at the same time. In other words, transnational movement and work occur across national borders, but they are not determined by those borders: instead, they can create new interstitial formations people and capital occupy and through which they transit multidirectionally.

In the context of higher education, where "international" projects may *seem* unidirectional—attracting international students; sending students to other countries for study; and importing/exporting curricula, faculty, and administrative models—a transnational analytic framework can reveal multiple directions, forms, and temporalities occurring and overlapping every day. Steven Fraiberg et al. (2017), for example, describe what they term the "translocal" classroom space at the campus in China where they were conducting research, in which students were fulfilling assignments from U.S.-based instructors but doing so by exploring issues that were locally relevant and current (p. 177). Danielle Zawodny Wetzel and Dudley W. Reynolds (2014) focus on their transnational campus, spanning the distance between Pittsburgh, PA, and Doha, Qatar. While their university's establishment of programs in the Middle East might appear on the surface to be a straightforward instance of applying U.S.-based instruction abroad, the authors claim that their first-year writing course provided exigence for bi-directional work. They leveraged the university's claim about sameness across the campuses to argue for curricular and programmatic change at the U.S. campus based on innovation in Qatar, thus reversing a traditional logic of curricular exportation from a "home" to a "branch" location.

At the Asia Campus, I observed and indeed helped facilitate a curricular export from the US to Korea. In addition to establishing outgrowths of academic major programs and staffing them with U.S.-based department-vetted faculty members, the university re-created a cohort model of first-year general education courses, requiring all students to take the same block of Writing, Introductory Psychology and Sociology, Math, and Global Citizenship.

Outside of the curriculum itself, the university's efforts to encourage Asia Campus students' identification with an emerging transnational social space were literally visible. On my return trips to that campus (which I describe more fully in Chapter 3), I noted that the brand-new classroom and office building my colleagues were occupying had been emblazoned with university logos inside and out in what appeared to be a very strong visual correction to the more spartan decorations of our first campus building. Photographs of the U.S. campus and of popular alpine and desert natural features of the Intermountain West were prominent in hallways. Furniture was keyed to university colors. And several rooms had been named after regional national parks. Those examples of investment in the university's symbolic presence reflected the institution's desire to create an "extended" rather than a "branch" campus—one that, like Wetzel and Reynolds' (2014) home institution, could credibly claim that students enrolled thousands of miles apart were nonetheless having the same educational experiences. In my university's case at least, "sameness" was symbolically imposed from afar through set curricula but also more materially through photographs, logos, color schemes, and other elements that seemed to pull students into a virtual social space heavily determined by their apparent destination in the US.

But as theorists of transnationalism would remark, the students were not *merely* pulled into such a space: instead, they were themselves co-creating it. As I believe my student participants demonstrated, they worked, lived, and interacted in ways that showed their "self-awareness of an imperfect foreign ear in an accentuated space" (Singh et al., 2007, p. 202). While all of the students who participated in my study were Korean nationals attending a university on Korean soil, as I will show, they acted overtly and subtly in response to their awareness that things were different at the Asia Campus than they would have been at the Korean university campuses very close by—and that they as students were often different from one another too (see, e.g., Brooks & Waters, 2011). In other words, there was friction just beneath the smooth internationalist surface of the university's and government's experiment that was both noticeable and variously productive.

Korea's Relationship with English and English Education

Given the location of part of my study site at a shared English-medium university campus in Korea, and given that country's significant investments in English-language education at primary through tertiary levels, I turn here to that country's history with the English language and the contemporary complexities in that relationship that inform my work. A significant part of that history includes Korea's simultaneous affinity for and suspicion of U.S. cultural influences—ambivalence that likely affects my university's campus there.

In widely circulating reports about international students studying in U.S.-based colleges and universities (especially the Institute of International Education's annual Open Doors report), Korea usually figures prominently as one of the top three sending countries—a remarkable position given that its population of roughly 50 million is significantly smaller than those of the top two sending countries, China (1.4 billion) and India (1.3 billion). Its disproportionate presence in international education is even more remarkable considering the relatively short history of Korean students' international circulation: Korea did not generally grant permission for its citizens to study abroad until 1980, before which only a very few highly privileged Koreans (most prominently the Republic's first president, Rhee Syngman) could pursue educational opportunities outside the peninsula (Cho, 2017, p. 70). Closely related, Korea's domestic history with English-language education and penetration also shows rapid recent development following a tumultuous 19th- and 20th-century history of international contacts.

Trade envoys introduced English to the Korean peninsula in the last quarter of the 19th century at a time when Korea became the last country in the region to be reached by prospective colonizers (Collins, 2005). The Empire of Japan was the most persistent regional force, and it attempted incursions into Korea beginning in the 1870s—efforts that led to the forceful imposition of a trade treaty in 1876. A combination of English-language trade emissaries' growing influences and internal fears about Japanese domination led to the creation of a dual-language (English/Korean) press and to the 1882 Shufeldt Treaty, which established commercial and diplomatic relations with the US. In addition to political and trade-based effects, JongHwa Lee et al. (2010) argue that Korea's opening to the US also encouraged Koreans to orient rhetorically to Americanization as an alternative to traditional Confucianism: while Japan would go on to colonize Korea between 1910 and 1945 (with social effects still readily perceivable in Korea today[4]), Japan's eventual defeat at the hands of the US became a powerful symbol of American economic and military might (also see Bizzell, 2017). Indeed, the ascendance of American "soft" (market-oriented) power after World War II was augmented in Korea by its

---

4   While there is evidence in Korea of an affinity for Japanese cultural artifacts, including art, design, and literary/popular productions, there is also an enduring strand of anxiety about and xenophobia toward Japan. Most visible is the ongoing dispute about the roles Korean women played during Japanese occupation as forced/indentured sex workers, or "comfort women."

"hard" (military) power. And both types of power were apparent in the U.S.-led postwar military occupation and in U.S. leaders' collusion with Korean elites (Lee et al., 2010, p. 347).

Since 1945, English's role in Korea has evolved from being the "language of the latest wave of occupiers" (Collins, 2005, p. 421) to becoming a language that represents a desirable, if somewhat conflicted, target for aspirational politicians, students, and parents (see also Cho, 2017, pp. 76–84). Korea remains among the most ethnically and linguistically homogeneous countries on Earth (Jeon, 2009), but English education represents a huge government and private investment. As Korea built its domestic economy after the Korean War of the early 1950s, and as interest in English (and U.S.-led globalization) grew, educational authorities attempted to shift English-as-a-foreign-language teaching from drill-based grammar-translation pedagogies to more communicative methods. U.S. Peace Corps volunteers were actively teaching in Korea between 1966 and 1981, and government investment in language education increased further as the 1986 Asian Games and 1988 Olympics increased Korea's international exposure. In the 1990s, as Korea emerged as "one of the most successful tiger economies" in East Asia (Jeon, 2009, p. 234), authorities revised educational programs pursuant to President Kim Young Sam's policy of 세계화 *(segyehwa)*, or "globalization": primary and secondary curricula integrated English education even further, and national standards specified that each school should have at least one native-English-speaking teacher on its faculty (Jeon, 2009, p. 235). Outside the school day, private tutoring centers marketed their services to parents, who seemed (and still do seem) eager to pay hundreds, if not thousands, of dollars per student per month for extra preparation in Korea's test-driven educational system. As Hyera Byean (2015) notes, parents felt compelled to pursue such private options in the wake of 1970s-era "equalization" policies that randomly assigned students to high schools and ended score-based tracking practices (p. 871). In a bid to win back affluent parents' trust in public schools, the Kim government reinstituted tracking, and the later Lee Myung Bak regime (2008–2013) entrenched tracking further and authorized more hiring of native-English-speaking teachers (Byean, 2015, pp. 871–872). Perhaps predictably, more tracking has meant even more familial private investment as parents use English cram schools to aim for the highest tracks, especially in high school English curricula (Byean, 2015, p. 873).

Thus the "English Fever" that grew apace with Korea's interest in globalization and that reached boiling after the Asian economic crisis of 1997–1998 has carried a high price tag (Cho, 2017; Park, 2009, 2012). Jin-Kyu Park (2009) relates that roughly half of all money spent on education in Korea in 2006 went to English-language preparation—a figure that translated to nearly $19 billion by 2009 (Lee et al., 2010, p. 338). Lee et al. (2010) cite further reports that as many as 40,000 Korean parents—mostly mothers—lived abroad in 2008, often in the US, as so-called "wild geese," supporting the children who traveled with them as they learned English in English-dominant primary schools alongside native-speaking peers. Perhaps the most compelling example of many Koreans' high investment in English proficiency is a trend reported in the *Los Angeles Times*, in which parents turn to surgeons to clip their children's frenula (membranes under the tongue), supposedly correcting tongue-tiedness and allowing easier pronunciation of unique English phonemes (Demick, 2002; also see Park, 2009).

Yet, as Samuel Gerald Collins (2005) and Mihyon Jeon (2009) argue, the assumption that Korea has unilaterally "bought into" English as a periphery nation adopting "inner circle" standards is unsafe: Korea is indeed continuing to invest in, adopt, and adapt to English but on its own terms. The growth of "Konglish" is clear evidence of English's evolution alongside the Korean language: many areas in and outside of the massive capital city, Seoul, are replete with advertisements including apparently direct/phonetic translations of English-language terms such as 핸드폰 ("han-deu-pon" / "hand phones" or mobile phones) and 소울푸드 ("so-uhl-puh-deu" / "soul food" restaurants), and the many and proliferating high-density apartment complexes can carry creatively elaborate English names that gesture to prestige, such as "First World" and "Hanwha Dream Green World Euro Metro" (Suk, 2015).

But the local and daily push and pull between languages is not the only evidence of Korea's adoption and adaptation of English: since English is closely associated with international trade, politics, influence, and education, its presence in Korea is also inflected by Korean desires to control it. There are instances of formal control of English teaching, as Jeon (2009) relates in her study of expatriate native-English-speaking primary and secondary school instructors who are heavily recruited but whose varied approaches can run afoul of centrally planned English curricula. There are also compelling examples of informal pressures to control Korean English that reveal ambivalence and anxiety—feelings I discovered among student participants in my study. Jinhyun Cho (2015) argues that Korea's investment in English is actually an investment in "linguistic perfectionism," a particularly intense regime of language assessment in which "even proficient speakers of English feel anxious" as they internalize critiques of their competence (pp. 689–690). Indeed, Adrienne Lo and Jenna Chi Kim (2012) observe that some reactions to the growth of Konglish itself have entrenched "racialized ideas of linguistic incompetency," in which Konglish and other putative evidence of substandard English skills are "framed as responsible for the country's low global status" (p. 259).

Even high levels of English competency, however, are not enough to allay such linguistic anxiety in Korea. In her scholarship on the status of professional Korean-English translators, Cho (2015, 2017) adopts Roger Goodman's (1986) anthropological distinction between "guknaepa" and "haewaepa" to discuss differences between Koreans who learned English largely in country versus abroad. In Goodman's original definition, guknaepa academics, who had earned degrees at elite Korean universities, felt competition with haewaepa, who had earned degrees at prominent institutions elsewhere. While Goodman (1986) noted guknaepa wariness about potentially unorthodox ideas among haewaepa, Cho (2017) argues that internationally educated translators in her study are more glamorous and desirable than domestically educated peers, owing to their pronunciation and their easier familiarity with international English idioms (p. 2). She relates the personal story of attending, as guknaepa herself, the most prestigious institute in the country for graduate-level translation studies and learning a key lesson about language, register, and globalization. She writes,

> I knew a lot of terms and idioms belonging to high-level English registers, such as "sabre-rattling" or "megaphone diplomacy," as we practiced interpreting with speeches delivered by officials and experts on global issues all the time. Having learned English through Korea's grammar-oriented English education tailored to university entrance exams, however, I occasionally experienced embarrassing moments when I did not know ordinary words such as "tadpoles" or "peekaboo," which overseas English learners had been exposed to in naturalistic environments. While I worked very hard to become a glamorous elite bilingual as projected in the media, I constantly desired the English language resources of haewaepa classmates and secretly wished that I had been given an opportunity to learn English overseas as a child. (Cho, 2017, p. 2)

Pressures of performance in the highly competitive and even glamorous orbit of professional translation are, in one way, certainly owing to the "ever-rising local standards for English skills" Cho (2015, p. 688) notes, but they are also owing to a different qualitative shift in "local standards" themselves that are less about higher and higher proficiency "scores" and more about the intensification (and personal internalization) of the regime of assessment that produces and evaluates such scores in the first place. As English maps onto social class and mobility, English-language competence becomes a moving target: Lo and Kim (2012) observe that newer Korean television dramas

("한국드라마"/*hanguk deurama*) depict cosmopolitan Seoulites flawlessly and effortlessly shifting among numerous languages other than Korean and English as if to reinforce the idea that real linguistic "competence" is a matter of carefully managing fluidity among several languages.

Faced with such formal and societal pressures to reinvent, both *guknaepa* and *haewaepa* can easily encounter discrimination and anxiety. *Guknaepa* may find their domestic preparation and credentials insufficient among other English speakers who have been privileged enough to travel/live/be educated abroad and/or in affluent cosmopolitan locations. But *haewaepa* may feel pressure to earn and keep their relative status and may feel effects of their perceived differences. Cho (2015) relates the comments of Soyoung, a research informant who left and then returned to Korea during the late 1990s rise of "English fever." As Soyoung recalled,

> I was like an alien. I am not a boastful character, as you know, and want to keep a low profile no matter what. But I received so much attention and I guess that girls in my [school] year all knew that I had lived abroad. . . . My Korean sounded funny and my English was awesome in their eyes and I was just an interesting subject. My English teacher always asked me to read English textbooks because he was ashamed of his pronunciation. (Cho, 2015, p. 699)

Ultimately, the attention that *haewaepa* attract as apparent models of "proper discipline," "hard work and education," and "complete mastery" (Cho, 2015, p. 693) can potentially position them as unique among some of their peers—an uncomfortable position in a country that values a high level of social cohesion.

Students in my study, coming from different educational backgrounds and bringing different kinds and levels of English proficiency but sharing Korean citizenship and heritage, seemed to imagine themselves as members of a transnational institution. They were on Korean soil for much of the term of my study but daily encountered people, expectations, and symbols that prompted them to create transnational social space at the same time their faculty members were creating it as well. When they did, they negotiated the parameters of that space through nuanced language work, including writing. Social and familiar pressures, desires for individual achievement, and awareness of the emergent nature of the transnational experiment combined and were refracted through the campus- and city-in-progress. In the next chapter, I describe that campus and city scene and my own encounter with it as a resident and researcher more fully.

2 WAC On Spec: A Critical Narrative of My Year at the Extended Campus

Given my close connection to and direct involvement in my university's extended international campus, I provide in this chapter a critical narrative of my mutually embedded professional and personal experience there.

The multi-university[5] Incheon Global Campus, the location where the University of Utah Asia Campus operates in Korea, is in turn part of the Incheon Free Economic Zone, established in 2003 in an attempt to attract tourists as well as foreign investment to the Yellow Sea ports closest to Korea's capital city, Seoul (Incheon Free Economic Zone, 2018). The campus is located in New Songdo City, a planned community with a target population of at least 250,000 that is built atop land reclaimed from tidal estuaries. The city includes a highly promoted business and entertainment district that is itself a $35 billion public-private real estate-based partnership between Korean and U.S. companies. As one of the city project's main architects describes it, the district is "a model for future, sustainable city-scale developments, not only in Asia but across the globe" (Kohn Pedersen Fox Associates, 2020). Where no artificial structures existed prior to 2005, an island containing at least 150,000 residents, offices for 1,600 companies, at least 1,000 retail or hotel businesses, the tallest building in Korea, and a Jack Nicklaus-designed golf course now provides evidence of astoundingly fast economic development and breathtaking financial opportunity, and my university is part of the vision.

Of course, living, working, and walking on the ground as a semi-permanent city dweller allowed me to develop different views. I had been primed to expect what an article in *The Atlantic* described as "a history-less and especially unnatural city . . . 'an ideal test bed,' as one Cisco employee put it, a massive blank slate" (Arbes & Bethea, 2014, n.p.). However, I came to know the city described elsewhere in the same article—one that was as subject to mid-decade economic downturns as much of the rest of the world had been, one in which the futurism of "smart" waste management systems "coexist[ed]

---

5   During the time of my study, Incheon Global Campus was populated by academic programs, faculty, staff, and students representing the University of Utah, the Fashion Institute of Technology, George Mason University, Ghent University, and the State University of New York at Stony Brook.

with the familiar and mundane" (Arbes & Bethea, 2014, n.p.; See Figure 2.1).
I came to know a city in which the many and proliferating steel-and-glass
towers, often empty but always well lit, reflected images of families and of
subsistence farmers growing vegetables in as-yet undeveloped plots (see Figure 2.2). I also came to know a campus and a university marked by the same
striking contrasts between huge and very human scales.

*Figure 2.1. Waste management machines in New Songdo City
next to bags of household/business waste. Credit: 'Future past
still in the making' by Kairus Art+Research, 2017. Kairus.org.*

*Figure 2.2. Large garden plot surrounded by new retail/
residential buildings in New Songdo City. Credit: 'Future past still
in the making' by Kairus Art+Research, 2017. Kairus.org.*

Indeed, while I was close enough to Seoul's photogenic density that I went regularly with my camera/smartphone, some of the most compelling pictures I took were in the still-sparse urban experiment where I lived and worked. To colleagues, friends, and family members, I described this place, the campus, and my university's role here as a "startup within a startup within a startup": it is a new institutional partner in a young educational experiment in a planned city that won't be finished until at least 2022. Most of the construction across the city was and still is "on spec," and I saw daily what that looks like: a lot of gapingly empty steel, glass, and concrete (see Figures 2.3 and 2.4). But it is slowly beginning to fill as both the campus and the city inch toward their target populations under the curious gaze of administrators, government officials, investors, and other stakeholders spread between cities 16 time zones apart.

Figure 2.3. Construction near Incheon Global Campus, August 2014. Credit: Author.

It is hard for me to think about my experience researching and supporting WAC/WID in Korea apart from the place itself. When I was asked to go to Korea, I knew I would be part of a very small initial group—small enough, in fact, that I was not only the entire WAC/WID program but also the entire writing center for an initial student body of fewer than 15. Both WAC/WID support and writing tutoring initially functioned out of my office, though I also started meeting students at the on-campus convenience store/cafe, because that felt a little less antiseptic. The extremely small human scale contrasted sharply, though, with the massive scale of the built environment, erected to accommodate thousands of students, instructors, and staff. The building into which we all moved to try to carve out our own identity away from another university's ubiquitous signs is a swooping, hypermodern semicircle—apparently the architect's idea of what a 21st-century global university ought to look like. We suddenly had cavernous new space to attempt to make our own. When I met cross-disciplinary colleagues for workshops on teaching writing, we gathered in a meeting room with a huge conference table and rolling/reclining executive chairs. (I felt as if we had broken into the boardroom, but no executives ever arrived to kick us out.) Our new building's design and scale made it seem like a broad canvas. But daily realities revealed the challenges inherent in an experiment of this kind—challenges that informed my own work. In turn, that complexity reflects the broader contexts of internationalization, globalization, and higher education I noted in Chapter 1.

Figure 2.4. Land clearing and construction on and near Incheon Global Campus, May 2016. Credit: Author.

In preparing to leave for Korea and in reading about the place while there, I encountered again and again visions of a campus and a city self-consciously inventing itself and projecting itself into the future—directly in line with Korea's clear desire to assert itself as a global economic power. My daily experiences, though, grounded those visions in inescapable multilayered complexities that permeated the educational experiment—including the teaching and learning of writing. Precisely due to such complexities, I offer this story of arrival, orientation, and encounter.

*Figure 2.5. Classroom/office building at Incheon Global
Campus, August 2014. Credit: Author.*

Early Days

Roughly a year and a half before my departure for Korea, the previous dean
of my college, who was part of a university-level leadership team coordinating
the international effort, had approached me to ask if I would be interested in
becoming one of the first faculty members to teach at the new Asia Campus.
Plans for majors and for the general education curriculum were still being
settled, and negotiations with the Incheon Global Campus Foundation and
the Korean Ministry of Education were ongoing, but the dean expressed his
desire that I commit to contributing expertise in second language writing. In
preparation for this opportunity, I agreed to team teach a learning community
course on global citizenship for first-year undergraduate students at the U.S.-
based campus. Shortly after I began teaching the first semester of that course,
the Asia Campus leadership team asked me to revise it for Korea on the
premises that all first-year students should take the same courses in cohorts
and that the theme of global citizenship was the best fit for the new campus,
its location, and its international population. Thus, when I was finally scheduled to travel to New Songdo City, I was contracted to teach not writing
but a still-experimental two-semester learning community course on global
citizenship, and also asked to create a writing center.

By this point, it had become clear to everyone that our inaugural class at
the new campus would be extremely small, which meant I would be teaching

one section of the learning community course instead of two. I used the preparation time freed by the cancelled section to design and give a presentation on disciplinary principles of assigning, responding to, and evaluating writing to a small group of faculty members who were scheduled to arrive in Korea at roughly the same time as me. My presentation was a basic overview that borrowed information from other presentations and from a general second language writing support site I had built several years earlier. In addition to presenting heuristic questions about what constitutes "good writing" in the undergraduate majors that would be offered at the Asia Campus (primarily communication and psychology, fields on which I will focus in Chapter 4), I described what we might expect in the writing of our second language (L2) English students based on research as well as on my own experiences teaching international students. I foregrounded Joy Reid's (1998) distinction between so-called "eye learners" and "ear learners," in which international students ("eye learners") typically learn English through grammar-translation exercises, and domestic second language learners in the US ("ear learners") often learn through daily interactions with native-English-speaking peers and from English-dominant media. According to Reid (1998), the differences in language learning backgrounds can mean that international students have high metacognitive knowledge of English-language grammar but not as much comfort speaking English spontaneously, while domestic L2 students may have speech that represents an idiomatic level of comfort but may find grammatical composition challenging.

Based on the knowledge that most of our first-time enrollees were from Korean secondary schools, I thus predicted that they would initially follow "eye learner" patterns. I also predicted that students would be highly attuned to writing as a form of testing given the highly cohesive standardized assessment environment in Korea, and so would require time to adapt to new and different academic expectations. I observed that their adaptation to/of the campus would necessarily occur alongside ongoing language acquisition, and that despite the traditional view of writing as the last of the "four skills" (in addition to listening, reading, and speaking) to be taught and learned, writing can and does occur while other language practices are developing. I concluded with advice on the utility of regular, low-stakes writing practice in and out of class times and a strong suggestion that faculty members provide models for the kinds of writing they were targeting. I cautioned that students may initially be reticent to ask questions in class because of perceptions of social distance and/or embarrassment about spoken proficiency. And I warned that the first-year writing courses we were planning to provide could not teach students everything they would need to know about how to write across the curriculum, especially since their enrollment in those courses would likely overlap with enrollment in somewhat more advanced/major courses given the small number of courses we could initially offer. As I'll explain shortly, our students turned out to be far more educationally diverse than I was predicting.

I arrived at the Asia Campus two weeks before the scheduled start of Fall semester. Five of the seven other inaugural faculty members had arrived; however, two were still trying to obtain Korean visas for their positions.[6] Meanwhile, the concerns that administrators and other stakeholders in the US and Korea had held about low initial enrollments were about to be confirmed: we would open at the beginning of September with a class of only 14, including two U.S.-based students who were officially studying abroad. Our small faculty, administrative, and staff cohort reflected the size of the student body. In the weeks before classes started, we all worked in an open office with cubicles, with the provost and I sharing one of them. Months later, long after we had settled into our own offices, I would joke with him that, in the first days, I worried that I was helping set university policy by turning sideways in my chair and expressing opinions to him. At the time, though, we were certainly involved in daily conversations that were clear expressions of our startup status, ranging from the best ways to coordinate textbook purchases to communicating with campus staff about challenges with classroom technology to discussing faculty cell phone contracts. When the other new faculty members arrived from the US, I was able to catch up with them about ideas for integrating assignment types and timing as well as content across courses. The writing instructors—a combination of experienced teachers with advanced degrees in either communication or linguistics—and I revised schedules between their first-semester composition course and mine so that students were writing summaries of a chapter about global citizenship just as they were practicing summary, paraphrase, and quotation. The sociology instructor—a faculty member from the university's College of Social Work—and I agreed to time our introductory

---

6   Visas proved to be a substantial logistical challenge. As a professor, I was granted a Korean E1 visa, which required employment verification but little additional documentation. Several instructors who did not carry the title "professor" were granted E2 visas, a classification that exists solely for employing language teachers (usually in secondary schools) from countries Korea recognizes as dominant sources of native speakers of the language to be taught. For instance, E2 visa holders seeking English teaching jobs must be citizens of Australia, Canada, Ireland, New Zealand, South Africa, the United Kingdom, or the US. Visa applicants must also submit to criminal background screening and sexually transmitted disease testing (https://www.korvia.com/e2-visa-korvia-guide/). There is no readily apparent relevant visa classification for university instructors who are not "professors."

readings about cultural diversity to complement each other. I discussed with writing instructors and with other faculty colleagues the advantages of coordinating reading and writing across courses in this way, starting with the required first-year writing courses. Colleagues outside writing reassured me that they appreciated my pre-departure workshop and my offers of ongoing support for teaching writing, but they were primarily invested in starting their own courses and communicating with their home departments at the U.S. campus. And in a couple of instances, they related to me that their courses were not particularly writing intensive anyway.

Learning Underway

At the start of the semester, several realities quickly became apparent. First, even though all students who were not coming from the US to participate in the learning abroad program were Korean nationals[7], they had more diverse educational backgrounds than my pre-departure introduction—or really any overview of "international students"—could have predicted. The majority had graduated from primarily Korean-language secondary schools in the country, but at least two students had lived and learned abroad in Canada, Thailand, and the UAE. Consistent with literature about Korean concerns over the deleterious effects of "too much" English learning, one of those students expressed to me on several occasions his anxieties about his Korean proficiency among peers and elders. Next, students were encountering problems with their online math course that became especially visible one morning as I walked into the classroom where I taught: several students had occupied the room the night before and had filled one large whiteboard with English-language math vocabulary. The challenge of tying ongoing language acquisition to conceptual knowledge of math was exacerbated by lingering problems with our university's course management system: the time zone difference had not been consistently set across all courses, which was creating deadline problems that were not quickly solvable given the asynchronous (email) communication on which students and their distant teachers had to rely. And the "writing center" that I had established was more of an idea than a visible support mechanism. While I had announced to faculty members and students that I would set aside hours per week for writing center consultations, I was often alone in my office as I observed that students were meeting with

---

7   The university initially planned on an eventual mix of 40 percent Korean national students, 40 percent students from other Asian nations, and 20 percent students from the US.

writing instructors immediately next door about assignments across their courses at least as often as they were meeting with me.

Outside of classrooms and offices, the startup nature of the overall campus project meant that lines among faculty, staff, and administrative activities remained blurry even after we moved into separate spaces. The extremely small initial enrollment placed a high premium on recruitment, and it also translated to the decision that our campus would enroll new students each semester for the foreseeable future rather than enrolling new students once per year. Pressure on the (small and new) recruitment staff was apparent as they traveled in and out of Korea, developed and refined marketing materials, and established relationships with well-known secondary schools—working through their own process of learning about how an IBC can and should position itself among other, much more established universities. On several occasions on and off campus (including a large national recruitment event at a shopping complex in Seoul), we faculty members participated in recruitment activities ranging from short speeches about our academic specialties to individual conversations with prospective students. On one hand, these were valuable opportunities to learn about students' and parents' expectations: almost invariably, revealing questions arose at each recruitment event about the value of "general education" and about the marketability of Bachelor of Arts versus Bachelor of Science degrees. To be sure, many faculty members may otherwise rarely encounter such questions once students are admitted and enrolled. On the other hand, recruitment felt uncomfortable. As Shun Wing Ng (2012) notes, intense competition for students in East Asia in particular means that faculty involvement in nonacademic activities is increasingly common—and that it can blur lines between academic work and globalization-as-business-enterprise as a result.

While I believed in the educational value of what we were presenting to students, I also knew that they and their parents might see a lag between what was promised and what had yet to be built. Indeed, the campus itself was a compelling symbol of that lag. As ground was broken on another new building into which my university colleagues would move, existing facilities remained incomplete, unoccupied, or unevenly serviced. Promotional videos about the campus that were displayed on a loop in our building's elevators showed a recreational pool that was unfilled during my entire year-long stay. An entire floor of our current building was unused, though signs on each door suggested the rooms' intended purposes. And the campus cafeteria regularly ran short of advertised items for lunch and dinner.

As the first semester progressed, we faculty began turning some attention to more specific planning for subsequent semesters. The next entering class of new students would likely exceed 60—significant growth that, we knew, would change current students' sense of cohort. To prepare, in addition to individual consultations/conversations with faculty, I led a brief workshop for all faculty that included sharing of student writing as heuristics for reactions and response. I also drafted a document based on the "Statement of WAC Principles and Practices" (http://wac.colostate.edu/principles/statement. pdf), in which I articulated both "learning to write" and "writing to learn" approaches, reiterated key second language writing concepts from my pre-departure presentation, and summarized the ongoing faculty development support I was interested in coordinating, albeit from the U.S. campus. That document included the first formal mention of the mixed-methods study that is the focus of this book.

Following a long break between fall and spring semesters, colleagues and I started classes in early March with a student body that was now greater than 70 and that interacted with student populations also of increasing size at the other universities operating on the shared campus. Oddly, I was not teaching any of the new students: the second semester of the learning community course I taught exclusively enrolled the now-second semester students. However, my writing center hours filled much more quickly than they had in the fall as students brought drafts of assignments ranging from weekly reading responses for their introductory communication course to mid-term APA-formatted essays for psychology. The diversity that colleagues and I had noticed among the initial cohort became even more apparent as the student population jumped: according to the survey I conducted that began the study that is the focus of this book, student respondents reported that they had at least briefly lived and been educated in at least nine countries outside of Korea.

In addition to the daily work of teaching and writing center support, I was looking ahead to returning permanently to the US and to attempting to maintain support for students and faculty from a distance. I tapped some funding for the small, shared campus library to purchase writing textbooks, style guides, and WAC/WID volumes as references for ongoing teaching. I met with and observed the writing instructor who would inherit the "writing center" from me and who would be responsible for setting up the dedicated tutoring space in the new academic building. In anticipation of conducting the research that led to this book, I read accounts of international WAC/WID programs and of longitudinal research on student writing, and I recruited a graduate student at the U.S.-based campus to return with me the following spring to observe and record faculty members teaching their courses and to interview participants. And I revised the pre-departure presentation on

WAC/WID and second language writing for the new faculty members who would arrive in late summer after I departed.

While I worked, I began to reflect on how the campus and its writing support might continue to develop, given the still-small human scale and the semester-to-semester changes, and given the experimental and ultimately uncertain nature of the entire venture. Each new group of students will change the student body quantitatively and qualitatively. The rapport that the initial faculty group developed, which seemed to be both an effect of the close proximity of office and living spaces as well as of the shared experience of simply being first on the ground, is not likely to sustain itself as the faculty complement grows and diversifies. And the administrative infrastructure will likely distance itself from both faculty and staff as it grows, too. Faculty colleagues willingly participated in WAC/WID activities and engaged me in conversations as we passed one another in hallways, hosted one another for meals, and traveled together to and from Seoul: I knew that kind of rich, informal interaction would be less likely after I returned to the US, even though I left materials and training behind and promised to stay connected via email and annual trips. Even if faculty commitment to integrated content/ pedagogies and principles of writing instruction were to sustain itself, I also worried, and still worry, along with my colleagues about what happens to literacy development during the long stretches between semesters. As I learned from literature on Korea's complex relationship with English and explored in Chapter 1, students who were Korean nationals were likely to listen to, read, speak, and write exclusively Korean during the months they were off campus, with little opportunity or incentive to continue the long work of acquiring the Asia Campus' dominant language of instruction. And looming over all was the agreement between the university and the Korean government, which codified the campus' status as a *startup* and reinforced the presence of its varied stakeholders.

A Promising, Uncertain Future

While it felt exciting and liberating to invent approaches to teaching and a range of other challenges based on our emerging experience, we knew that whatever we built faced the hard limits of funding as well as the vagaries of new administrators' decisions. It also faced and still faces the challenges of creating a sense of shared investment across two very different campuses separated by 6,000 miles. Before my departure and well after my return to the US, I spoke to faculty colleagues and community residents on and around the U.S.-based campus who had no idea that the Asia Campus existed—or who knew it did but who did not understand it. So in keeping with the uncertainties surrounding many other IBCs, the one where I lived and worked and with which I remain closely involved may yet fold. In Korea, it remains unclear whether the government's vision of ten universities with 10,000 students on the new shared campus is reachable, and it also remains unclear how much more funding it is willing to invest to maintain and enhance facilities for an international university that represents educational philosophies for which many Koreans feel ambivalence.

The university, the campus, the city are all part of an expensive, extensively advertised effort to market Korea as a canvas for investment, innovation, and international connection. But the canvas is actually a palimpsest: the massive utopian scale of speculative construction is offset by the local complexities inherent in any meeting of multiple cultures. Faculty members bring expertise and expectations tied to disciplines. Students respond to the pitch that attending a U.S.-based university in Korea gives them an international education in a key global lingua franca, and parents appreciate that that education does not require sending their children abroad. As both a new and willing faculty member and an expert on writing, I was able to observe what international education "on spec" looks like in a very specific way, and I have been able to argue that while writing is certainly a thread that ties curricula together, it is also, unavoidably, a site for teaching, learning, and administering that reveals gaps between idealized internationalization on one hand and concrete realities on the other. Whatever the outcome of this educational experiment, I have hoped to maintain a balance between eager participation and critical awareness.

3 Researching a Transnational Startup: Site and Methods

In the previous chapter, I provided a narrative of my experience at the Asia Campus from preparing for departure to returning to my university's U.S.-based campus. As I have stated, the complexities of the Asia Campus, New Songdo City, and the nation of Korea during this period of its rapid internationalization argued for a detailed description of my personal experience as a teacher, scholar, quasi-administrator, and resident. In this chapter, I take a step back specifically to describe the transnational site of my study—really, two campuses of a single university separated by roughly 6,000 miles—in terms of its student population, academic programs, and international aspirations. I reintroduce the research questions that arose from my experience at the Asia Campus and from my familiarity with relevant scholarship. I then describe the mixed methodological approach that informed my analysis of the range of data I collected from student and faculty interviews, faculty writing prompts, students' writing assignments, and the formal and informal observations research assistants and I conducted in and out of classrooms.

The Two University Campuses

The University of Utah is the largest publicly supported university in the state. In August 2014, when the Asia Campus opened, the total enrollment was roughly 31,000 undergraduate and graduate students. Among undergraduates, communication and psychology—the only two choices of major available to Asia Campus students during the time of my study—were and remain among the top ten majors by enrollment. Over the last several years, and indeed since my own arrival as a faculty member at the U.S.-based campus in 2006, the university has been highly academically aspirational.

One clear expression of such aspiration is the university's investment in internationalization. In 2010, the university entered a public-private partnership with an international pathway program, a partnership that lasted until 2014. While that effort to recruit and retain a larger number of international students was not a perceived success (see Jordan & Jensen, 2017), the university engaged a new private partner in 2018 and began allocating new revenue from the partnership to dedicated courses, advising, and campus space. At the same time, the university's Office for Global Engagement consolidated several units, including International Student and Scholar Services and Learning Abroad, into shared offices and sought to unify international projects.

But probably the most visible international project has been the Asia Campus—the university's first campus outside the United States. As I mentioned in Chapter 2, Utah is in fact one of five U.S.- or Europe-based universities currently participating in Incheon Global Campus (IGC), a project that represents a $1 billion investment from the Korean government to create a "global education hub" in Northeast Asia (Incheon Global Campus, n. d.) that would attract highly regarded international universities to grow intellectual capacity supporting public and private investments in biotechnology. Early discussions among U.S.-based university officials, Korean alumni, and Korean educational authorities, however, revealed interest in humanities and social sciences curricula as well (M. Hardman, personal communication, October 22, 2020). Negotiations eventually led to the creation of the Asia Campus as an "extended" campus of the university, initially housing three undergraduate degrees—communication, psychology, and social work[8]—and a master's degree program in public health. Undergraduates were intended to spend three years taking a combination of general education and major courses before transitioning to the U.S. campus for a final capstone year, though the timing of that transition has varied somewhat based on students' plans, academic performance, and ability to relocate. Those academic programs are part of a larger social and economic scene reflecting not only the university's but also Korea's aspirations, as I explained in Chapter 1. Korean student writers—as all rhetors—bring to any communicative task a collection of consciously manipulated and unconsciously inherited affordances and constraints shaped by competence, experience, affective orientation, and motivation. Capturing and analyzing that multidimensional collection would be difficult with the best possible methodological tools. It is impossible through textual analysis alone.

Methods

My familiarity with relevant scholarship and my awareness of the role writing would play in the extended transnational campus curriculum prompted an initial set of writing- and pedagogy-focused research questions:

- How is writing being explicitly and implicitly taught in courses across the curriculum at the new campus?
- What kinds of writing are instructors assigning across the curriculum?

---

8   The social work major stopped operating during my study due to low enrollment.

- How do students perceive/respond to the writing assignments and teaching?
- How do instructors respond to the students' writing?
- What effects do students' transitions from the international campus to the U.S. campus have on their own and their instructors' perceptions and responses?

While those questions consistently guided interviews and my analyses of other data about writing, I understood from the beginning of my study, as I have noted, that the complexity of that writing's "context" made it impossible for me to isolate writing from its surrounds. Thus, I added this question to my initial list:

- How does writing as a privileged literate activity reveal the relationship between internationalist claims about education and the daily lived complexity behind such claims?

Given my need to balance analysis of students' already complex negotiations with writing on one hand and sensitivity to the emerging "context" on the other, I employed a range of qualitative methods intended to uncover nuances of students' and instructors' motivations, perceptions, and experiences. Methods included the following:

- A ten-question survey of all Asia Campus students in Fall 2015 (roughly 110 students total at the time), which asked about backgrounds and experiences in speaking and writing in English as well as about the kinds of writing they were already doing or that they anticipated doing in their majors (See Appendix A.)
- A three-question survey of all eight Asia Campus faculty members in Fall 2015, which asked about writing assignments and preoccupations in responding to student writing (See Appendix B.)
- Eight 46–60-minute in-person, semi-structured follow-up interviews with select students at the Asia Campus, co-facilitated by research assistants,[9] conducted in May 2016, 2017, and 2018; informal post-interview discussions of initial analyses with research assistants; and three additional in-person interviews with students after their transition to the U.S. campus (See Table 3.1.)
- Seven 30–45-minute in-person, semi-structured follow-up interviews with select faculty at the Asia Campus, also co-facilitated by research

---

9   Graduate students Justin Grant Whitney in 2016 and Charissa Che in 2017, and undergraduate student Joanne Castillo in 2018

assistants, conducted in May 2016, 2017, and 2018; informal post-interview discussions of initial analyses with research assistants; and three additional in-person interviews with Asia Campus-based faculty members visiting the U.S. campus (See Table 3.2.)

- Collection of 71 student participant-provided examples of course writing ranging from brief reading responses to final semester projects
- Collection of approximately ten examples of faculty-provided syllabi and writing assignment prompts/descriptions
- Classroom observations and audio-recorded post-observation debriefing sessions conducted with research assistants during the May 2016, 2017, and 2018 Asia Campus visits

I used initial student and faculty surveys to begin identifying themes to explore further in interviews. Of 110 student surveys distributed, I received 20 completed responses—a low response rate potentially reflecting my own departure from the Asia Campus to return to the US and/or some fatigue from other more official university surveys about academic programs and student life. Eight students who had completed surveys responded positively to my subsequent email message asking whether they would be interested in a follow-up interview as well as additional visits, interviews, and collections of their writing/ faculty responses to their writing over the next two to three years. Ultimately, five students committed, although, since one of the five withdrew from the university in 2016 for health-related reasons, I followed four students throughout my study.

Table 3.1. Student Participants

Student Participant	Dominant Language(s)	Major	Gender	Other
Alice*	Korean (self-identified first language)	Communi-cation	F	Korean secondary school bkgrd, 3 months' study abroad in Canada
David	Korean-English bilingual in speech, more self-iden-tified English proficiency in writing than Korean	Psychology	M	international school bkgrd (Korea), father from US, dual Korea-U.S. citizen
John	English with increasing Korean proficiency (both parents Korean)	Psychology + Social work	M	school in several coun-tries, including Canada and UAE
Jane	Korean (self-identified first language), English learned only in Korea	Psychology	F	secondary school in Korea only

All participant names are pseudonyms.

Table 3.2. Faculty Participants

Faculty Participant	Department Affiliation	Campus Location	Gender	Other
Professor W	Communication	Asia Campus	M	U.S. educated, native English speaker, originally hired at U.S.-based campus
Professor M	Communication	Asia Campus	M	U.S. educated, native English speaker, originally hired at U.S.-based campus
Professor A	Psychology	Asia Campus	F	Korea and U.S. educated, native Korean speaker, hired at University of Utah Asia Campus (UAC)
Professor B	Psychology	Asia Campus	F	U.S. educated, native English speaker, hired at UAC
Professor O	Writing & Rhetoric Studies	Asia Campus	F	Turkey and U.S. educated, native Turkish speaker, hired at UAC
Professor K	Psychology	U.S. Campus	F	U.S. educated, native English speaker, hired at U.S.-based campus
Professor E	Psychology	U.S. Campus	M	U.S. educated, native English speaker, hired at U.S.-based campus

Of the eight initial faculty surveys, I received four complete responses: one faculty member replied to my emailed cover note that he and at least a couple of his colleagues were not teaching enough writing in their courses to warrant their potential inclusion in my study. Based on the faculty surveys that were returned, I invited respondents (Professors W, M, A, and B) who were then teaching courses enrolling my student participants to meet me for initial and follow-up interviews. As the study progressed, I identified Professor O, who was working with one of the student participants in an independent study I describe in Chapter 4, as well as Professors K and E—based at the U.S. campus—to whom other faculty participants directed me as U.S. campus instructors whose courses enrolled relatively large numbers of post-transition Asia Campus students.

Approach

My approach is guided by tenets of grounded theory (GT; see, e.g., Bowen, 2006; Charmaz, 2003, 2006; Glaser & Strauss, 1967). I have found GT especially valuable for this study given its explicit aim—to develop descriptive theories that, as the name implies, are grounded as much as possible in daily experiences and the ways participants make sense of those experiences implicitly and explicitly. Contrary to quantitative researchers' claims that qualitative work was biased or even idiosyncratic, Barney Glaser and Anselm Strauss together and separately articulated an approach that *grounded* credible theory building in the simultaneous and recursive collection and analysis of data from live phenomena and processes. GT's openness to emergent codes and themes in naturalistic settings and its skepticism about established theoretical categories allow me to balance scholarly understandings of multilingual writing on one hand with the discursive and material complexities of writing's scenes and contexts on the other.

In my recursive readings of surveys; interview transcripts; student writing/ instructor responses; notes from classroom observations; and other material describing coursework, writing assignments, and instructional/other campus spaces, I employed "open coding," in which I tagged data with preliminary candidate codes arising from my experiences as a teacher of second language writing at both the U.S.-based campus and Asia Campus, from my knowledge of the relevant scholarly literature, and from my desire to remain sensitive to students' and faculty members' emic perspectives on their academic and social interactions. As interviews, other data, and interactions with research assistants generated more candidate codes, I began to shift my analytical focus to what grounded theorists term "axial coding," in which I analyzed additional data with the goal of confirming, disconfirming, and/or consolidating emerging codes as I approached a point of diminishing returns. Chapters 4 through 6 report on my analyses and explication of several of the most durable emergent themes. (See Appendix C for the full list of codes.)

I have been inspired and informed by a number of prior studies of writing that are more explicitly and clearly longitudinal than my own (Beaufort, 2007; Carroll, 2002; Chiseri-Strater, 1991; Haas, 1994; Herrington & Curtis, 2000; Smoke, 1994; Spack, 1997, 2004; Sternglass, 1993, 1997; Wardle, 2007; Wolcott, 1994; Zamel, 1995). But I have come to realize that my study has diverged significantly from these as well, given that maintaining consistent contact with the scene of my research—the site and the faculty and student informants—presented significant challenges. Of course, my study is not unique in that respect. Marilyn Sternglass (1993, 1997) acknowledges, for instance, that keeping in touch with student participants in particular can be frustrating since students are generally relatively transient. Even now, two and a half decades after Sternglass' data collection, when students have more durable phone numbers and other contact information thanks to the proliferation of digital communications, I was not always able to stay connected with all student participants. And my physical distance from the Asia Campus for most of the study period meant that my impressions of the scene came in fits and starts as the campus and surrounds were quickly evolving. Unavoidably uneven data collection can exacerbate some of the problems Richard Haswell (2000) observed—in a strident critique of longitudinal work—problems including not only small and relatively unstable participant groups but also a lack of comparable writing tasks and conditions. Haswell went on to criticize longitudinal researchers as well for relying on open-ended interviewing and "intuitive evaluation of course writings" (pp. 310–311).

If the goal of writing research is to produce readily generalizable results that may serve a comprehensive theory and one-size-fits-all pedagogy, Haswell's (2000) concerns are merited. However, qualitative writing researchers have long argued for the value of their work in providing unique insights grounded in site-specific conditions that are not transferable but nonetheless valuable to the field's accretive—story by story and layer by layer—understanding of composition as an inescapably social and material practice. Lee Ann Carroll (2002), for example, explicitly rejected "explanation, prediction, and control" in favor of a loose approach oriented to understanding the phenomena she was observing as closely as possible.

Moreover, some compelling scholarship on transnational education affirms the value of methodological complexity. As I noted in Chapter 1, transnational subjects cultivate identities and practices that are pushed and pulled among overlapping spaces: students in my transnational university may spend most of their undergraduate careers at a campus geographically located in Korea, but they are embedded in social, discursive, and material ecologies that remind them of the U.S.-based campus' symbolic proximity and its temporal inevitability given students' requirement to travel there for a year of study. That institutional push and pull, the physical campus' and city's constant hypermodern rate of change, and students' cultivation of what Peggy Levitt and Nina Glick Schiller (2004) term "multilayered and multi-sited identifications in and across local, regional, and national spaces" (pp. 8–9) call for especially sensitive empirical approaches. As Fraiberg et al. (2017) term it, situating writing as a literate activity in a global framework requires "fine-grained tracing of mobile literacies across space-time while connecting moments of everyday practice to wider distributed networks" (p. 19). Thus, again, this work requires balance—between capturing the development of writing teaching and learning across an institutionally determined transna-tional scene and timeframe on one hand and capturing the richly accret-ing detail of that scene on the other. While Brice Nordquist (2017) notes that educational initiatives are often predicated on "predictable repetitions of movements of people, objects, texts, ideas, and information" (p. 9), the projected outcomes of such routines run up against the embodied experiences of both researcher and participant.

That confrontation, for Nordquist (2017), between smoothly articulated claims about educational progress and the complexity of actual lives-in-education has immediate relevance for scholarly representations of literate activity in motion. I did not and could not have overlooked writing's embeddedness in the densely layered symbolic, material, and social context of my transnational site—not as a resident of the campus and city nor as a faculty member and informal administrator nor as a researcher who left and returned repeatedly to re-encounter the memory of my lived experience there. All were entangled. But my study's reflection of that entanglement, I hope, enlivens "context" as it interplays with other data and analyses of "writing," revealing the fecundity of a transnational educational experiment that, on its surface, can still seem smooth, future-focused, and predetermined.

4

Grounding "Transfer": Writing in Two Disciplines in a Transnational Ecology

Relevant literature on writing across the curriculum, writing in disciplines, and knowledge transfer can helpfully articulate how field-specific goals and expectations can translate to writing teaching, but there are gaps in that literature that must be filled in practice and on site—especially where faculty and students feel an acute need *both* to teach and learn a discipline *and* acclimate to various broader educational and social characteristics of the institution. My university's transnational context is no exception. The small number of major degree programs offered at the Asia Campus represent that campus'—and the university's—main academic identity to students and their parents. While staff members and even, at times, faculty colleagues and I felt a need to "sell" the concept of general education courses to potential recruits and their families (since there was little analog at established Korean universities), we felt equally strongly that students and families were looking to affirm what they believed true about the value of U.S.-based degrees—a belief reinforced by the Korean domestic marketing of the Incheon Global Campus. There seemed to be clear expectations among students about what the degree programs were supposed to set as targets for them—the production of peer-reviewable research reports, ethical and authoritative news stories, and actionable public relations campaigns.

At the same time, there is at least some ambivalence in the disciplines represented by student participants' majors about the extent to which the teaching of writing is supposed to introduce and reinforce formal genres and styles on one hand and/or facilitate disciplinary thinking and socialization on the other. In addition, at the Asia Campus and at the U.S.-based campus to which students transition for roughly their final year of study,[10] faculty members demonstrate clear allegiance to their disciplines, but they also show clear attempts to anticipate and respond to the linguistic and intercultural

---

10   The original Asia Campus plans called for students to spend three years in Korea before transitioning to the U.S.-based campus, where they would finish capstone coursework and participate in commencement ceremonies. In practice, some students have negotiated earlier transitions in order to take a wider range of courses at the U.S.-based campus than is offered in Korea.

complexities that mark both campuses of their transnational institution. Further, my observations and field notes suggest that the Asia Campus itself was functioning as an actor: much more than a backdrop against which primarily academic activities were occurring, the evolution of the campus' and the surrounding city's own space seemed to shape faculty-student interactions and students' writing in nuanced ways.

This chapter focuses on ways students and faculty members participating in my study at the Asia Campus and U.S.-based campus oriented to one another and to the ecologies in which they were embedded—with particular focus on how that ongoing orientation influenced and is influenced by the role writing plays in disciplinary identities. As students write to learn and learn to write (predominantly for my student participants in the fields of communication and psychology), they arguably "transfer" knowledge and practices from one course to the next and from one campus (in Korea) to the other (in the United States). But transfer is never linear nor a matter of straightforward transport and reuse: instead, the knowledges and practices transferred are sticky. That is, they show evidence of a given writer's learning and emerging experience while also tracing what Kevin Roozen (2009) refers to as the ontogenesis of the "literate subject" (pp. 567–568)—a coming-into-being that cannot but include many of the ecological factors relevant to the kind of complex, emerging site my university represents.

Indeed, in such a site, transfer is unavoidably inflected by the dynamism, idiosyncrasy, cross-contextualization, rhetoricity, multilingualism, and transformation Michael-John DePalma and Jeffrey M. Ringer (2011) argue are especially characteristic of second language writing. Thus, this chapter counterbalances arguments about transfer and about WAC/WID in communication and psychology with ongoing grounded analysis of the data within the "transnational social space" (Faist et al., 2013) that extends across my university's two campuses.

Double Shift: Writing in Communication at the Asia Campus

At UAC, writing in the communication major emphasizes critical thinking, ethical action, and closely edited newsworthy text production. That balance reflects some of the broader field's interest in articulating a dual role for the communication degree, and especially the mass communication/journalism emphasis—both as an investment in liberally educating undergraduates and in training professional documenters of news and social trends. (See Blom

& Davenport, 2012; Deuze, 2001, Eschenfelder, 2019, Massé & Popovich, 1998; Smith, 1997.) As do students in the journalism emphasis at the U.S.-based campus, Asia Campus students take courses in newswriting and in feature/magazine writing as soon as practical after finishing general lower-division writing courses. Students also take required courses in media and society and in mass communication law. This range of courses and genres is apparent in faculty participants' writing demands. For example, students in Professor W's media ethics course were writing their own codes of ethics following guidelines and models from the Society of Professional Journalists—augmented by Professor W's provision of explicit rubrics. However, Professor W did not provide rubrics for newswriting since, as he related, discussions about content and format occurred in class and editorial meetings (interview, May 2016).

The assigned writing in Communication also reflected faculty-student negotiations in an emergent, multilingual "transnational social space" (Faist et al., 2013): language-related challenges combined with other characteristics of this small startup that was functioning as both part of an established university and as its own smaller-scale experiment. That is, as instructors and students negotiated the pedagogical scene, they were also negotiating material affordances and constraints that shaped their interactions and prompted creative responses. As scholarship on English education in Korea demonstrates, many students graduating from domestic secondary schools likely encounter substantial shifts upon entering U.S.-style introductory writing courses. My anecdotal familiarity with the communication major's newswriting course (at least at the U.S.-based campus) and my knowledge of scholarship on mass communication pedagogy (see, e.g., Leggette et al., 2020; Massé & Popovich, 1998; Panici & McKee, 1996) prompted me to believe that students would have to shift *twice*—from narrative and even explicitly creative writing to the argumentative and expository writing featured in the university's general first-year writing courses, and then once again to the specific generic and style exigencies of AP-formatted news reporting. When I expressed that concern to U.S.-native Professor W (interview, May 2016), he concurred briefly but then related that he had contacted several students he knew would be enrolling in his introductory newswriting course the following semester. Relating that he believed they were all "a little bit nervous about it," he then described some specific details about his planned course scheduling and delivery in ways suggesting both his anticipation of some language challenges and also his creative thinking about the affordances of a small student cohort and relatively straightforward overall course scheduling.

43

W[11]: I'll just be teaching one, one class a week instead of two. And then Thursday, so I'm still deciding, I'm probably going to discuss with the students whether we do Monday, Wednesday, Thursday, or Tuesday, Wednesday, Thursday, but they'll have their class on, you know, the two sections will have their class on Tuesday, the other section will have their class on Wednesday, and then Thursday I'm just in the lab all day long. And I'm just going to say everybody has to come in here for at least two hours sometime during the day, I don't care when it is. You can split it up, you can come for an hour in the morning, hour in the afternoon. I've already been through all of the other schedules to make sure that everybody has a

Jay: There's a two-hour block there for

W: And everybody can fit in two hours those days. And I've already looked at, kind of, whenever all the other classes are, and there's no reason that you would have a schedule that wouldn't allow you to fit in two hours.

J: And you're just going to camp out in the lab.

W: I'm camping out in the lab. And the idea is you're working on your articles, you're making columns, you're doing what you need to do to make sure, and basically we have a newsroom type of setup.

Thus, students' relatively constrained course selection meant Professor W could identify "open" blocks for most, if not all students and could create "a newsroom type of setup," in which he would lead a traditional lecture-and-activity meeting one class day per week but then alternate with open time during which he would act as a newsroom editor. Such a setup not only approximates a paradigmatic social/professional scene in journalism—predicated on field-specific insistence on explicitly socializing students into journalistic practice (see, e.g., Smith, 1997)—but also permitted Professor W, in his words, to have "a little more of a capacity to oversee the work that's being done" given his concerns that students were synthesizing existing writing rather than writing their own reporting:

---

11   All transcriptions use minimal markup provided by the professional transcriber. Deletion of end punctuation indicates at least some overlap with the next utterance. Ellipsis on an otherwise blank line indicates the exclusion of at least one line of quoted transcripted speech.

One of the things that I'm running into a lot right now is it's so hard to convince these students that they need to not just read a bunch of articles and then just sort of summarize it into their own article. That's not really what journalism is. But they do it over and over again. They say, oh, I said I ask them, "where did you get that information from?" and they say, "oh I read it in an article." So then it's not cited right, and frankly, we really don't, you really don't want to cite to some other news article. That's just not the way that journalism works.[12]

As Professor W implies, the more focused newsroom setup could facilitate time assisting students with the shift away from introductory academic synthesis and summary toward reporting. That time, in turn, would no doubt be facilitated by the built environment of the campus itself, on which living, recreational, and instructional spaces were only a brief walk apart from one another.

Magazine Writing, like the newswriting course, presents Asia Campus students opportunities for journalistic writing. Given the rapid evolution of the city-scale experiment in which UAC is embedded, there are certainly possibilities for creative reporting, including opportunities to write features, review new businesses, and profile students and faculty members. However, there were challenges in the course, similar to those in Newswriting, related to style, format, and teaching approaches. In a May 2016 interview, Professor M implicitly alluded to the same substantial shift from students' academic to more professional writing that Professor W noted, claiming that students have "been taught to footnote everything, and you don't footnote on articles: you just say it." In fact, the double shift I noted above that Korean students often need to make from secondary-level writing to first-year expository and argumentative writing and then again to professional writing may be even more pronounced in the magazine course. In describing his approach to teaching students about diction and tone, Professor M related that he advised students to "focus on trying to write the way you speak":

---

12   There are some strident claims in mass communication scholarship about the field's protection and advancement of credibility, ethics, and free speech (Blom & Davenport, 2012; Smith, 1997). Those claims warrant wider claims about what Edward J. Smith (1997) refers to as the overlap between an ideally trained journalist and an ideally liberally educated student: identifying an exigent topic, developing a point of view, and contextualizing that perspective among others, in Smith's view, are simultaneously the best ways to write a story and the best ways to achieve critical thinking.

I tell them just, you know, you actually speak very well. And in fact, you've been talking since you were two years old. But writing in college for only about six months. So if your speaking ability has surpassed your writing ability for now. So if you just try to communicate that way, it'll be easier, it'll flow more smoothly, and this will be a good tool. So that's been good. I tell that to people in the, um, in the American student body as well. . . . There is kind of learning curve to figure out that they can do that, it's safe and they'll be better.

The advice to "write the way you speak" may seem to Professor M like an intuitive way to reduce students' anxieties about composition in the profession, but it was not as likely to evoke the same colloquial knowledge of English among Asia Campus students as it would at the U.S.-based campus. Indeed, given what I related in Chapter 1 about pre-university English education in Korea, many Asia Campus students are more familiar with formal, less colloquial expression. Student participant Jane's discussion of learning magazine writing, for instance, revealed some concerns about her own transition:

Jane: Formats, kind of, I have to . . . it's kind of hard for me. Like, we have to start with capital letters but the larger box, and I have to write in three columns, and I have to like blurb.

Jay: Yeah, write a blurb, like a really short statement.

Jane: And I have to, mm, umm, I don't know how to say, but I have to write in my own ideas except like, citation thing.

Jay: So you said citation thing, but you put your fingers up to show quotation marks. Do you mean quotations, like you're . . .

Jane: Not the quotations but citations.

Jay: So what kinds of citations are you supposed to do in magazine article writing?

Jane: Um, like someone says something like, actually I'm doing a restaurant review right now, but I went to a restaurant with my friend . . . and I put some kind of decorations and like, pictures, and my picture as well.

Jane's description of her writing tasks was relatively disjointed, but it was evident that she found challenges both in understanding some of the particular formatting requirements (which are less constrained by a standard such as AP than they are in newswriting) and in understanding how sources (in this case, a friend) might be represented in relatively informal writing. Again, Professor M's advice that students can and should write the way they speak did not seem natural to Jane.

At the same time, student participant Alice's response to journalistic writing and editing made visible some different kinds of familiarity and suggested nuance among students' levels of comfort with rhetorical demands of the field. In a visual editing course taught by Professor W, Alice was one of the editors—responsible for selecting, polishing, and including stories written by fellow students in what she described in a May 2016 interview as "my newspaper." Despite her position as a class editor, though, she expressed discomfort resulting from her perceived abilities with formal written English:

> J: What does the editing consist of? What are you doing when you are editing?
>
> A: So, grammatical mistakes, and news stories have to have some important elements. For example, leads. So for the first paragraph, we are supposed to um, have like five W's, like *where when why who, why*, something like that. So, we try to edit that when we read other students' stories. If that's missing, we edit that. We add leads, and also try to edit the entire, like, flow.
>
> J: Okay, so like flow, cohesion, so you add like transitions and stuff like that.
>
> A: Yeah, it's really difficult. Especially when it's second language. I don't even know if I'm writing it like, correcting right or not.

In other ways, however, Alice was demonstrating much more confidence as she moved between genres, reflecting the field's attempt to balance formal/academic and informal/popular generic expectations. In two versions of her news article about U.S. President Barack Obama's 19 September 2015 weekly radio address, for example, Alice clearly adopted the succinct AP style she mentioned in her in-class editing role. In a terse, single-sentence first paragraph, Alice concisely reported the "five W's" of Obama's speech, relating that the president "discussed the remarkable economic growth of the United States following the 2008 financial crisis and called for the Republicans in Congress to pass a responsible budget"—a sentence that she had revised from an earlier two-sentence paragraph. Between versions, there was more evidence of very close editing for AP style, including the reduction of participial phrases ("in his September 19 weekly address" for "in his weekly address given on September 19") and inversion of attribution phrases ("said Obama" for "Obama said").

Even more of Alice's genre sensibility emerged between her newswriting and her magazine feature writing, as her article about Korea's high-stakes national university entrance exam exemplified. In keeping with Professor M's advice to "just say it," Alice's style and tone were far more conversational than in her newswriting:

> On November 12, 2015, South Korea came to a grinding halt due to a singular event. Suneung, the life-changing college exam. Many parents were praying for their sons' and daughter's success in the exams in front of exam halls. As 631,100 high school seniors were taking the most important exam of their lives, even the skies above Korea have gone silent. Even the skies above Korea went silent.[13] The government stopped flying aircraft to reduce noise, and it ordered public offices, major businesses, and the stock market to open an hour later than usual Thursday for students to avoid traffic jams. . . .

> That's right, all of this happens for test, specifically, Suneung, the life-changing college exam given to Korean students in their senior year of high school. The exam comes around just once each year, and nearly everyone in Korea is impacted. Many parents (stand?/kneel?/linger?) outside of the exam halls, praying for their sons' and daughters' success.

Here, on a topic Alice and most other Korean students would find personally relevant and highly memorable, Alice used a combination of vivid and adjective-laden description, repetition, and conversational strategies ("That's right") to emphasize the importance of *suneung* and attempts to maximize the resources of writing for a popular feature.

As Alice's and Jane's work illustrate, writing in communication courses at the Asia Campus was a balance among students' adaptation through a double

---

13   In Chapter 1, I related information about Korea's exam-heavy educational culture. My critical narrative in Chapter 2 as well as my and my research assistants' observation notes from research visits include numerous mentions of sound— large trucks and other construction/earth moving equipment, wind, and popular music coming from loudspeakers at a construction site next to our campus. Seoul, where research assistants, colleagues, and I often traveled, always seemed loud and rushed in many locations. So Alice's repeated description suggests how remarkable enforced silence on exam day can be.

shift—from "creative" secondary school writing to prototypical "academic" writing in introductory composition to complexly multi-register proto-professional writing in the major. It was also a balance negotiated by faculty members, who clearly demonstrated allegiance to in-field ideas about journalistic writing as well as writing for other academic/professional purposes in communication, but who also felt the exigencies of their multilingual and transnational context. In a May 2017 interview, Professor M mentioned that he had shifted his focus in Magazine Writing to emphasize visual design over equivalent time on close language editing since the new focus seemed more fun and more familiar for students and since "even the best students are really not going to be real top of the line writers in English."[14] In the same interview, Professor M also discussed a mass communication law course that he and Professor W, both attorneys by training, regularly taught. While both faculty members were aware of the university's and department's directives to make the Asia Campus curriculum closely mirror the U.S.-based campus', they recognized the limitations of teaching U.S. case law in Korea. But since neither was an expert on applicable Korean law, they defaulted to textbook-heavy instruction predicated on the U.S.-based law with which they were more familiar, and which the vast majority of communication majors overall would be expected to know anyway. Their attempts to adapt in both journalistic and more theory-heavy courses exemplified the push and pull necessary to build a curriculum grounded in academic and professional considerations and simultaneously responsive to local resources and constraints.

High Stakes and Affective Investments: Transnational Writing in Psychology

As in the communication curriculum, psychology students and faculty members were balancing disciplinary goals with the need to account for everyday

---

14   Professor M's approach reminded me of experiences colleagues and I had had teaching the small initial group of students during the Asia Campus' first year of operation. In the global citizenship course I taught, my co-teacher and I integrated assignments requiring students to use their ubiquitous smart phones to take photos of objects they owned as part of an audiovisual presentation about the globalized supply chains that supplied those objects to them. We also engaged students in using their phones virtually to "tag" images of places on and around campus as part of an assignment on global street art and activism. While Professor M did not explicitly scaffold his shift to visual design the same way colleagues and I scaffolded the smart phone-based assignments in the other course, the similarity exemplifies this transnational social space's interrelationships between teaching/learning and the broader ecology.

linguistic and cultural differences in their transnational setting. Students' writing in the psychology major at the Asia Campus before their transition to the U.S. campus reflected disciplinary and faculty expectations about personal interest in relevant topics tempered with an emerging understanding of the field's dominant genres and styles. It also reflected anxieties about linguistic performance in writing under at least some pressure from perceived expectations of the U.S. campus—a campus that, as I related in Chapter 2, was symbolically present at the Asia Campus in the curriculum as well as in the images and icons that consistently oriented students and faculty to the broader university. In a May 2016 interview with Jane, I asked about differences she perceived between her magazine writing course and the psychology research methods course she and other students were taking—a course required for all psychology majors and an elective for all students.[15] In contrast to the informal—even conversational—writing she and Alice reported in communication courses, writing for her research course immediately seemed more explicitly thesis driven: as she reported,

> we have to do, writing headings, subheadings, and everything. Introduction, methods, and results. We have to write three parts and within those things we have to write a participants, measurements, and how, yeah, how are we going to recruit participants and compensation.

In several interviews with multiple students and faculty members at both the Asia Campus and the U.S.-based campus, the themes of writing as a means to learn to think like a psychologist and of writing as a means to record and display research results were pervasive—and reflective of claims in psychology's literature about the utility of WAC/WID-based "writing to learn" and "learning to write" approaches. (See, e.g., Friedrich, 1990; Goddard, 2003; Hettich, 1990; Jolley & Mitchell, 1990; Madigan & Brosamer, 1990.) Students paid significant attention to the requirements of the introductory research methods course Jane discussed. Similar to the communication major's newswriting course, this course seemed intended to expose students to preferred research genres, styles, and formats as soon as possible after first-year writing. Indeed, a social work professor who was one of the inaugural faculty members at the Asia Campus assigned significant low-stakes writing in both

---

15   There was significant crossover of student enrollments during and after my own year at the Asia Campus: it was common, given the small faculty complement and relatively limited course selection, for psychology students to take communication courses and vice versa.

her introductory psychology and sociology courses but also insisted that students learn and practice APA format[16] and include explicit introduction and conclusion sections—anticipating the more closely formatted research articles students would read and begin to write. Overall, then, students in the psychology major consistently encountered writing assignments geared toward their early intellectual and professional development; however, those developmental goals were at times inflected with the dynamic histories and cultural/linguistic investments that critical transfer theorists observe.

One required psychology course—Research Methods—was especially noteworthy for the academic and professional stakes it held and for the reactions it evoked. During my academic year at the Asia Campus, the course was not taught. With additional faculty hiring the next academic year (2015–16), the course came online—and it quickly acquired a reputation for rigor. The centerpiece and the major assignment of the course was an IMRAD-formatted research paper[17] on topics students were permitted to choose but for which the instructor provided fictional data. Through the semester, students submitted, revised, then resubmitted each discrete section, beginning with an introduction that included references to literature. In successive interviews, Professor A, the Korean- and U.S.-educated faculty member who taught the course at the Asia Campus during my study, described her approach as well as her perceptions of student work in terms emphasizing a combination of disciplinary and idiosyncratic expectations—the combination of which revealed very high and even personal stakes for Professor A's identification with her students' ongoing language acquisition. In May 2016, Professor A observed a range of problems with student writing:

> A: not only the grammar, grammatical errors I had to keep
> on telling what to do but also about overall structure. How
> you develop your idea of message. Because you need to use the
> backup research saying probably it's not ready about your topic
> of interest. And then you should have the section of what is

16   Psychology's sense of ownership of American Psychological Association (APA) styles and formatting is on display in relevant literature, in which a students' APA adherence might seem to be a close analogue to their field-specific reasoning ability. In a report of a psychology professor's collaboration with a writing center consultant (Miller & Andrews, 1993), both tutor and instructor consistently direct a focal student back to an APA handbook for authoritative guidance ranging from the length of an abstract to the actual content of a discussion section.

17   Following an organization that includes discretely labeled sections for an introduction, methods, results, analysis, and discussion.

> not known, so that your research can contribute. But then they were not getting that.
>
> J: Yeah
>
> A: But the biggest points off was from the quoting.
>
> J: Mm
>
> A: They were quoting. In psychological research, we don't quote, we cite.
>
> J: Yeah, you're just citing, you're just paraphrasing, summarizing, and citing, right.
>
> A: In terms of the ideas and findings. But they were missing that part, a very huge part.
>
> J: That's interesting, they do
>
> A: They were just quoting the results.
>
> J: Yeah
>
> A: Like, depressed people were doing this. Quoting, just no no no.
>
> . . . A: So it is the curriculum, right, learning about it is what we need to do during the course of study so I shouldn't worry too much. But then the papers were shockingly disorganized.

In ways similar to many U.S.-based faculty as reported in literature and through anecdotes, Professor A discussed several generic, conceptual, and stylistic considerations that overlapped. While concerns about grammar arose several times during my interviews with her, Professor A was quick in this excerpt to note apparent problems with "overall structure," by which she meant a common and privileged arrangement in research article introductions through which a writer reviews "backup research," observes a gap in that research, and turns to their own contribution. Her attention to structure was consistent with psychology literature that advocates for teaching empirical report writing to introductory-level students as an opportunity to "help [them] see that this style communicates the logic of the scientific process" and that the preferred report organization "mirrors the ideal research process" (Goddard, 2003, p. 28; also see Miller & Andrews, 1993).

Indeed, Professor A's qualification that "learning about it [research and writing in psychology] is what we need to do during the course of study" represents her implicit recognition that students continue to learn psychology-based literacies throughout their majors. And in a comment that was unusual among faculty participants in my study, she alluded in a May 2018 interview to a broader need to coordinate with first-year writing instructors and the campus' writing center, reflecting a shift from the initial faculty cohort's relative disinterest in such coordination that I reported in Chapter 2:

> We [UAC faculty] don't have the agreement on the level of expectations. From writing center, and writing courses, as well. So my expectation for the persons who have completed successfully, by getting A from Writing 1010 and Writing 2010, would be this [gestures with flat palm parallel to floor], but they are here [makes same gesture slightly lower to floor]. I mean, I'm talking about those who got A's, right? But then, where is this discrepancy from? So we need to communicate from within our faculty members first, so that we could channel students to get the proper help, or assistance, or guidance in the proper timing.

However, beyond that implicit curricular criticism that is relatively common in WAC/WID literature and in anecdotal experiences, Professor A's comments were also sharply evaluative and even carried attributions of emotional states to students. Beyond observing that students' apparent lack of conventional organization and their tendency to quote from literature were generically inappropriate, Professor A related her feeling that "depressed people were doing this." While I did not ask her to elaborate and would not want to speculate on what that statement could mean, it is clear that Professor A's response to at least some student writing carried a strong affective charge. As a U.S.-educated Korean national and native Korean speaker herself, Professor A was unique among faculty participants, and she suggested her background and experiences prompted her to identify with the Korean students who were in the vast majority at the Asia Campus. Thus, the disciplinary goal in which Professor A was clearly invested—namely, to teach students empirical logic through writing—and the institutional imperative to prepare students for upper-division coursework with primarily native-speaking faculty members at the U.S. campus were arguably sharpened for Professor A by her high personal investment in preparing these particular students at this campus.

Students too were highly invested, concerned, and at times frustrated—especially with the research course—as they encountered different/contradictory feedback while they worked their way through the curriculum. In May 2016, Jane related the clear difference between her first-year writing class and the research class, noting that while the earlier course required students to write proposals for papers and support theses, it was comparatively "lenient" because their theses did not have to be "valid" and because every sentence they wrote did not have to "sound perfect and professional." In a May 2016 interview, student participant John responded to my question about feedback he was receiving in the course by describing what he called "harsh" responses:

> Like, grammatical mistakes, like punctuation errors, um, when we were missing something like a page number for APA format. Like, that would deduct points. Um, some people, er, in my case too, I forgot part of an introduction completely and that would, like the title page, I forgot to do that. So the grading is not—I wouldn't say necessarily on the content but on the formatting issue.

David's May 2017 response to a similar question about feedback focused more on the content of his writing than on grammar and formatting, though he also suggested that the course was exacting:

> [Professor A] assumes that she doesn't know anything, so she'll be like, explain to me more, in detail. She likes, she likes details and to be more specific, and giving examples, and stuff like that. She usually doesn't give an answer but kinds of leads students to find an answer by themselves. . . . For example, if a student say, um, "household status," for example, that is sort of vague. But for the students, they already know what is household status to them. But Dr. [A] assumes she doesn't know anything about what they mean.

While students' and Professor A's responses about effective writing in the research course's high-stakes major assignment ranged from clear conceptual information to organization to page numbers and other format details, that range does reflect to a large extent disciplinary investment in writing. Using writing as a way to teach students how to "think like psychologists" is a common goal in psychology pedagogy (Boice, 1990; Dunn, 1994; Goddard, 2003; Miller & Andrews, 1993; Zehr, 1998; Zehr & Henderson, 1994), and the balance of concept, argument, support, synthesis, formatting (especially in APA), and style that was apparent in Professor A's responses to writing showed her interest in writing as a technology for making students' emerging thinking vividly apparent, as she stated:

> Knowing the whole research process, and by writing, meaning, in their writing, it should be conspicuous that they understand the whole process, and that they have concluded, in that pro-

cess, to have the outcome, right? . . . as a writer, as any writer, the reader should follow their thought processes, and that should be integrated in their writing. (May 2017)

Professor A's grading rubric assigned 30 points to "organization and structure," 30 to "APA style," 30 to "language," 70 to "improvement" from initial to final drafts of each research article section, and 40 to "originality." Students reported that they were more or less free to select topics, which tended toward Korean issues: in the research course and then in a summer group research project facilitated by Professor A, Jane focused on physical child abuse in Korean families and on Korean student stressors, respectively. In fact, Jane explicitly discussed her positionality—and specifically her motivated topic choice—in her group project, writing that "as a Psychology BS majoring student, I wanted to study why particularly college students in South Korea have more job seeking stress."

However, aside from brief mentions of topic selection in interviews about and/or writing samples from the research methods course, "originality" (with respect, for instance, to topic choice) rarely emerged in collected data despite the relative weight that criterion had in Professor A's rubric. There definitely appeared to be more emphasis on conforming to generic conventions and deploying field-specific terms. Jane's introduction to her final draft research methods paper began with a United Nations definition of "child abuse" complete with APA-formatted reference. After mentioning the recent emergence of several new protective laws, Jane shifted in the second paragraph to what she saw as a gap in child protection in Korea, noting that "investigations into factors of child abuse performers and therapeutic intervention towards them are insufficient." In her portion of the group-based summer research paper on students' stress, Jane followed a similar organization, including some literature review/synthesis in the introduction. She also adopted some preferred stylistic conventions in her brief report about methods, though the shift from her author-evacuated statement that "participants of this research will be recruited within the [Asia Campus]" to her more personalized claim that "my participants' inclusion criteria will be very specific and international" showed evidence that her familiarity with the subgenre of the methods section was still developing.

Beyond the introductory methods course and related writing projects, psychology majors encountered assignments that allowed them to work somewhat more creatively and personally, though faculty expectations that they use the assignments as opportunities to "think like a psychologist" remained consistent. A social psychology course at the Asia Campus included a "research paper" assignment that combined reinforcement of textbook psychology concepts (for instance, conformity, obedience, and persuasion), critical review of relevant experiments from literature, and an opportunity for students to speculate about further research on the topics—all within a highly structured assignment that required APA formatting and style. A cognitive psychology course, also at the Asia Campus, required a similar structure but encouraged students to reflect on how their thinking was changing through new concepts: Jane's "thought paper" on language, for instance, included her experiences with patterns of interaction among students from Korea and the US interspersed with references to concepts from intercultural communication. I had personally witnessed a broader conversation among students who were debating the utility of an "English only" policy on campus to ameliorate what they believed to be low proficiency and a lack of English-language interaction, so Jane's paper was evidence of disciplinary practice tied to sensitivity to the linguistic complexities of her surrounds.

As students transition to the U.S. campus, the combination of personal/academic/professional motivation and their emerging disciplinary knowledge becomes even more vital. Interviews with U.S.-based campus faculty participants revealed an expectation that advanced undergraduate students begin to specialize in the field, shifting from class-based proto-professional writing assignments to higher-stakes tasks—an expectation that seemed to prompt both students and faculty to contact one another across the campuses in order to establish relationships and explore options. However, even more attention to writing does not necessarily translate to more attention to the close stylistic and formatting expectations students would have focused on extensively through Asia Campus coursework. In an April 2018 interview in her office at the U.S.-based campus, Professor K related that she was in consistent contact with pre-transition students interested in human factors-related study and work[18] and that she was advising them to take a specialized writing course with her while they were connecting with potential faculty mentors:

> It's more of the technical writing, so they'll have to sometimes write amendments to our ethics board. So, really having to kind of follow a very specific structure of these different sections, and then they write a—what ends up being a five-page, single-spaced conference paper. . . . They are actually submit-

18   The APA describes human factors and engineering psychology as a specialization that "focuses on improving and adapting technology, equipment and work environments to complement human behavior and capabilities" (see https://www.apa.org/action/science/human-factors/education-training).

ting data, analyzing data. I mean, it depends on what the project is, and the nature of it, but basically we want to be able to
say by the end of that project that they have human factors
experience from start to finish. Here is a writing sample that I
can offer to potential jobs or graduate schools.

At the same time Professor K was facilitating advanced writing in the
discipline, students had ideally identified a mentor from among psychology
faculty and had attached to the project and lab that mentor leads. That connection then involved students in submitting study-related documents to the
Institutional Review Board (IRB) and in creating actual conference proposals. At that stage, students' writing as well as their interactions with mentors
began to reveal the graduate student-faculty mentor interactions Jay Jordan
and April Kedrowicz (2011) noticed in engineering labs, in which significant
time and attention were devoted to quick-turnaround publications, such as
research articles, conference proposals, and grant applications, intended to
advance specific academic projects and even support the labs themselves.

Interestingly, as students' writing after their transition to the U.S.-based
campus aligned more closely with faculty/lab projects, the attention faculty
members such as Professor K paid to formatting and style was somewhat
attenuated by broader goals of socializing all psychology students into a community of psychologists—goals that seemed to position writing as a medium
through which students could and should circulate their ideas, seek responses,
and build relationships:

We don't expect people to have done this type of writing very
often. So we try to really prioritize in that upper division
[writing course] a lot of feedback. Like, don't sit there and
beat your head against the wall for an hour. Write something,
give it to me, and I will say like what's on track and what isn't.

To be sure, as Professor K also related to me, she was concerned that students adopt recognizable professional styles early, and she found herself advising students to prune writing that may show their personal investment in and
understanding of relevant topics but that was too conversational. Professor
B, also in a 2018 interview but at the U.S.-based campus, introduced similar
concerns about students' overly informal tone and also about their tendency
to include too much written "filler." For her, there can be a particular premium on conciseness when writing for academic and professional journals:
hard limits on word counts and space can mean the difference between the
acceptance and rejection of article submissions, despite their overall quality.

Thus, U.S. campus-based faculty members I interviewed, generally aware of disciplinary standards and individually aware of the constraints on their own professional writing, counsel students to write "correctly," but they do so in view of the role writing plays not only in training students to "think like psychologists" but also in view of the socialization necessary to sustaining psychology communities. That is, despite some of the pressure Asia Campus faculty and students seemed to feel about connecting technical correctness in writing to disciplinary knowledge, U.S.-based faculty participants seemed at least as interested in writing as a way to facilitate necessary relationships with more expert psychologists.

Discussion

Students in my study learned and adapted dynamically and even idiosyncratically as they negotiated language contact in an academic and broader transnational scene that pushes and pulls. Adapting to the same transnational scene, their faculty members established and enacted disciplinary expectations through writing but also through a range of activities with which writing interanimates. So both faculty and students reflected Leki's (2007) conclusion that writing may be most important not as the academic/disciplinary coin of the realm but as an important though not unique means of "disciplinary socialization" (p. 245)—a finding of Leki's that is sharpened by the particular kinds of socialization and ecological development of my site. Communication students often encounter news/magazine writing courses that require them to write in explicitly journalistic styles on tight deadlines designed to reflect the pressures of a newsroom environment or editorial collective. However, those environments are also laboratories for students to socialize, trying identities, routines, and habits of critical questioning that are key skills for reporters—but also key to what many communication scholars believe is the process of learning how to be civically engaged. And psychology students may become collaborators on research projects and associated IRB protocols, articles, conference papers, and grant proposals even as undergraduates, but literature on psychology pedagogy also values students' writing that is personal, exploratory, and experimental for its own sake. Indeed, an additional faculty informant in my study, Professor E, related that he asks students in his U.S. campus-based introductory cognitive science course (which enrolls students who started at both the Asia and U.S.-based campuses) to analogize between visible structures (such as a sculpture in the university's art museum or the traffic patterns along a major off-campus thoroughfare) and the brain structures he teaches.

An artwork or roadway that invokes a brain structure, a classroom-turned-newsroom that creatively manipulates contact hours in the ways Professor W did, the shift to more visual composition/editing as a way to reduce students' anxieties about correctness in Professor M's class—all may work for students as instances of the boundary objects or cultural tools Kevin Roozen (2009) and Elizabeth Wardle and Roozen (2012) discuss. In making sense of his focal student's trajectory of writing, Roozen (2009) observed that Angelica held onto longstanding personal and expressive literate practices despite negative feedback about her application of those practices to academic writing about literature. Her persistence paid off in a journalism course, in which a teaching assistant (TA) advised her that all good writing is actually revision of existing text and practices. In addition to appreciating Angelica's own perseverance, it is useful to appreciate the persistence-in-evolution of her literate activity itself in ways Roozen (2009) suggests: the "object" (to use the sociocultural vocabulary circulating in at least some transfer literature) remains sticky enough as it is "handed" across contexts that it facilitates literacies while it also traces an ontogenesis of the "literate subject" (Roozen, 2009, pp. 567–568). Thus, the tendency of some traditional transfer research to imply that individuals carry knowledge/practices from one context to another and reapply them in predictable ways is insufficient to net the wide range of potential actors/objects, including the anticipatory actions and adaptive reactions of faculty, programs, majors, and institutions (cf. Yancey et al. [2014], p. 10).

The need for such an ecological perspective to trace the ontogenetic characteristics of literate action is especially clear in the transnational site of my own study. As I relate elsewhere in this book, it quickly became impossible for me to disentangle my own embeddedness in the overlapping material and metaphorical ecologies of the Asia Campus from my intention to study writing across the curriculum: in grounded theory-inflected terms, that embeddedness was a "sensitizing concept" (Blumer, 1954; Charmaz, 2003) that may have operated as a boundary object for my own writing. Relevant to thinking about the ways faculty members and students in communication and psychology were building and replicating literate communities, I see patterns of literate development that cannot but reflect transnational complexities. Similar to the negotiations Soomin Jwa (2019) observes her Korean focal students making as they shift from first-year to advanced business writing, I noted students' making "educated guesses" based on their perceptions of a "broad range in application of the concepts and skills" they learned earlier (p. 116). Even though Professor W warned students about what to expect in journalistic writing courses, they still needed to adjust on the fly, with varying degrees of comfort: Jane found some of the generic conventions of magazine writing unusual, and Alice expressed clear discomfort as a second language "editor." But Alice applied her personal investment in Korea's exam-heavy culture to vivid writing about national testing, and Jane arguably developed some genre meta-awareness because she was constrained to take both newswriting and psychology methods courses owing to the small number of courses offered at the time. While several students found writing in psychology highly challenging and at times exacting, they tended to use the opportunity to write for formal and less formal purposes as ways to make sense of daily concerns around the campus and community, such as language/interactional differences with other students and the stresses of academic achievement among Korean youth.

Faculty (re)oriented themselves around these literate actions as they applied field-specific writing pedagogies reflected in literature and, in many cases, in previous experiences teaching at the U.S.-based campus. But they also revised and refined those approaches as they recognized transnational complexities. The still-small student population and limited course offerings afforded Professor W the chance to block "newsroom" time each week in his course, and Professor M refocused work in his magazine writing curriculum to visual design, thus temporarily reducing his more usual emphasis on close language editing. While Professor A's comments pointed to significant affective charge around her reactions to psychology students' writing, that investment arguably showed her keen awareness (as a native speaker of Korean herself) that Korean-speaking students may have a higher bar to clear with written expression as they work toward capstone courses at the U.S.-based campus. However, Professor K expressed more interest in Asia Campus students' socialization into lab settings and into collaboration with mentors over drafts in progress than she expressed in grammatical or format correctness on arrival.

It is difficult to conclude with specific instances of *what* transferred and *how* from course to course and campus to campus. Rather, my analysis of specific details around the writing of student participants majoring in communication and psychology reinforces Jwa's (2019) call for attention to the *ways* of transfer. That kind of attention is not only qualitative in nature but necessarily open to the list of characteristics DePalma and Ringer (2011) assign to "adaptive transfer": dynamism, idiosyncrasy, cross-contextualization, rhetoricity, multilingualism, and transformation. That list resists direct programmatic or curricular direction, instead prompting research and teaching that hold in balance the exigencies of academic and professional genres, students' histories and rhetorical work, instructors' nimbleness and investments, and the ecologies in which all those considerations interrelate.

5 Beyond Coping to "Natural" Language Work

Literature in second language writing points to a range of ways to theorize what Leki (1995) referred to as "coping strategies." In that study, Leki collected data around five student-participants' responses to writing tasks, which ranged from clarifying the demands of writing assignments to relying on their native/home languages to resisting teachers' demands altogether. In perhaps the most telling comment in Leki's study, her student "Ling" demonstrated her awareness of cultural/linguistic difference and her simultaneous desire to employ such difference productively:

> [T]he strategy that Ling used most effectively was taking advantage of first language/culture by relying on her special status as an international student. As the semester went on, she attempted to incorporate something about China or Taiwan into every piece of writing she did, saying, "I am Chinese. I take advantage." Thus, her term paper in Behavioral Geography became a comparison of Taiwanese and U.S. shopping habits. Her term paper in World History became a comparison of ancient Chinese and Greek education and this despite her history professor's direct request that she not focus yet again on China. In this case she used a combined strategy of resisting the professor's request and of reliance on her special status as a Chinese person, and it worked. (Leki, 1995, p. 242)

As Leki's term has circulated in scholarship, the concept of "coping strategies" has provided valuable insight into the creative ways students can exceed predefined limits imposed on them because of their putative language limitations. Maybe the most infamous cases of L2 students' running up against such limits are instances of so-called "plagiarism," a concept that writing scholars have critically questioned for decades in attempts to articulate various rationales for students' textual borrowing apart from unproblematic claims of "cheating" (see, e.g., Currie, 1998; Howard, 1995, 1999; Howard et al., 2010; Pecorari, 2016; Shi, 2004).

But while "coping" through imitation seems more positive and less academically or ethically fraught than "copying," the term risks reinscribing deficit-laden implications that second language writers act with agency primarily, if not exclusively, in response to intransigent faculty demands and rigid academic and disciplinary expectations. In other words, the term suggests not only that students can perhaps *only* "cope," but also that instructors and faculty members can *only* create inflexible assignments and evaluation/assessment mechanisms that necessitate students' coping.

My study suggests that students can and do act with considerably variable competence, and it also suggests that the ground for that competence is extremely nuanced and capacious. Despite conventional and scholarly assumptions that Korean students demonstrate monolithic characteristics (including filial and social conservatism as well as a lack of spontaneous procedural knowledge of English), I have encountered students whose backgrounds, experiences, goals, and implicit awareness of the transnational campus' unique material and rhetorical affordances and constraints demonstrate surprising diversity. I have also encountered faculty informants who creatively negotiate their expectations, balancing a clear desire to support students' disciplinary understandings on one hand with engaged interest in how academic work is done under pressure in a transnational context on the other hand. Thus, incorporating student and faculty interview responses, information about writing tasks at both the Asia and U.S.-based campuses, and my own observations, I focus in this chapter on instances of "coping" that index not only students' adaptive responses to writing/speaking tasks in their majors but that also hint at broader entanglements of assigning and doing writing in a complex transnational ecosystem. I argue that instead of creating and simply reacting to staid academic literacy demands, faculty members and students alike aim for what one student participant describes as "natural" language work developing within their emergent shared context.

Campus Ecologies and "Natural" Language Work

The Asia Campus is a ripe site at which natural and artificial ideas about place, nationality, and conditions for education are in flux. As I related in Chapter 2, my university's campus, the larger shared campus, and the city all appear to compose a smooth site for transnational education at which what Wilkins and Huisman (2012) describe as "isomorphic" educational models might be transferred from the U.S. campus. On the ground, there is no such smoothness. U.S.-based cultures of higher education—ranging from administration to progress toward degree to our collective assumptions that "participation" in class can and should mean "individual speech"—interact daily with analogous Korean cultures that stress administrative distance from faculty and students, distance *between* faculty and students, and high national/collective investment in English language learning. The mix is visible and otherwise sensible on a daily basis, and it has required students and faculty alike to adapt creatively.

Researching Comfortable Language: Alice's Adaptive Negotiations

I focus here on one student participant who demonstrated a range of perception and adaptation given her multimodal and multi-genre relationship with English. Alice was a Korean national in her late 20s who majored in communication from her enrollment at the Asia Campus in 2014 until her 2018 graduation. She attended Korean primary and secondary schools throughout her education and traveled briefly to Canada during high school. She has been and remains active on social media—especially Instagram and YouTube, where videos and images show evidence of her interests in travel, food, and differences in the ways Koreans and Americans interact. Like many of her peers, Alice found the dual adjustment from high school English courses (which emphasized grammar and routinized speaking over writing) into the required first-year writing courses at the Asia Campus—and *then* from those courses into gateway news- and magazine writing courses in the communication major—highly challenging. An additional course on public speaking prompted anxiety as well, despite Alice's clear comfort with English speech in person and online and despite the commonality of public speaking contests in Korean middle and high schools.[19] In this excerpt, Alice related her response to a speech assignment her professor clearly intended to be extemporaneous that shows evidence of what Leki and other scholars might well call "coping," including direct resistance to her instructor's admonition not to memorize. Beyond merely a reaction to that requirement, though, Alice's strategy appeared to be a productive example of her ongoing attempt to make her English speaking more natural:

> A: Ever since I took the public speaking class, it was Professor W's class, that one was a tough one. Cause he wouldn't give us an A if we tried to read from the paper. So I have to memorize the whole speech. I had to. To get an A. So I did it for every speech.
>
> . . .

---

19   Several other colleagues and I were asked to judge such a contest, hosted by Incheon Global Campus for local middle school students. We were directed to score and rank speakers on categories including English pronunciation and grammar.

He made a speech competition, like [our] students, [another university's] students, yes, and I had to go there to just get an A. And for that, it was also long, it was an eight-minute speech. So what I did was I wrote the whole script and then I read it several times and then without script, I started giving a speech with my, what, recorder? And I, of course I would make mistakes. Whenever I would do it, I stopped that, and I'd listen to what I say and I'd do it again and again and again and finally I memorized the whole thing. I think it's also because I hear a lot what I'm talking about. Myself.

J: So you say the speech into the recording, you listen to it, and then you

A: Yeah . . . So I don't think, cause even Professor W didn't know that I memorize the whole thing.

J: Really, he thought that you were

A: Nobody knew that I memorized the whole thing. People thought that I was actually doing it spontaneously.

Considering that the instructor had asked students to speak extemporaneously—not reading or memorizing—Alice's memorization was definitely legible as the kind of resistance Leki's student, Ling, showed. To be sure, Alice was highly motivated by assignment and course grades, and her perfect GPA at graduation was a clear symbol of her desire to, as Leki's student, Ling, put it, "take advantage." But Alice also showed complex awareness of and adaptation to other, less obvious considerations.

Several of the interviews I conducted with faculty informants (including a couple who would have been teaching public speaking) revealed that instructors are keenly invested in teaching students disciplinary conventions while simultaneously guiding them toward less formal academic and professional environments than students had perhaps been primed to expect. A graded extemporaneous speech is an example of that attempted balance. And Alice's response to it was to avoid the need to read the speech aloud by memorizing it extensively enough that she could credibly deliver it "naturally"—even seemingly extemporaneously. Her recursive recording, listening, and memorizing resembled a strategy Xiao Lei (2008) noted in studying advanced English majors in China: her student participant Henry described his tendency to "extract some beautiful sentences and words from literary works, keep them in [his] notebook, review, recite, and remember them," using them selectively in his own writing. He went on to relate that sometimes the expressions "pop[ped] up in [his] mind" as he wrote (p. 224; see also Mu & Carrington, 2007). As Henry and Lei's other informant, Jenny, reported, they could feel "temporarily immersed in an English environment while living in a Chinese-speaking society" (Lei, 2008, p. 225). Like Lei's students, Alice created an English environment for herself comprising expressions she could repeat and rehearse to a point at which they seemed familiar—natural.

Indeed, Alice's awareness of the importance of "natural"-seeming comfort with English even in academic or professional environments inflected her tacit definition of "research," a term that my student and faculty participants may have mentioned more than any other. Reflecting some of the same emphasis on memorization that Alice discussed for her "extemporaneous" speaking, her research comprised material relevant to the topic at hand but also material that was generically and stylistically similar to her expected product. That is, Alice creatively used requirements/opportunities to do "research" as ways to expand her generic, stylistic, and lexical storehouse.

> A: I think that writing well is, for students who are using their second language, I think research skill is actually different. So when I try to write my paper, I try to read it, just read news stories that are, even though, I mean . . . that are related to or not related to the topic I'm about to write. So that I can be prepared with my writing. And I think that's, that's research. No? Because it's really hard for us to create our own expressions. Cause it won't be natural.

> J: OK. You mean written expressions.

> A: No matter how we try, yeah.

> J: Why do you think, you said that research is especially important for students who speak English as a second language. Why is it especially important for students like you?

> A: Because without research skills, um, you won't achieve the, you won't be able to write what you want to write. I think whenever I try to write something, I try to find similar writings. I mean, similar expressions.

> J: So similar to the type of writing you want to do?

> A: Not—even though when the writings are not related to my topic, at all, there might be similar expressions that I want to write.

J: You're reading the sources that you feel you need to read in order to do the research. But then you also read other things.

A: Other things too.

J: And how do you find those other things if they're not related to the topic?

A: I would maybe read textbooks or magazines. I don't know, and like, I just um skim through it and if I find similar expressions, that I want to write, I use that and after I do it like once or twice, it kind of, I can kind of memorize it so that I can use it again. It's not much problem later.

Alice here related her adoption of an autodidactic method that foreign language teachers have long advocated—that is, reading whatever you can get your hands on in the target language. In studying Korean high school and university students, Kyoung Rang Lee and Rebecca Oxford (2008) noted similar approaches. Where their high school student informants memorized and/or dictated expressions they encountered in relevant language learning materials, university students apparently felt freer to use more entertaining content, such as music, film, and magazines, and they in some cases imitated favorite English-speaking actors or attempted to predict upcoming lines of dramatic dialogue.

Interestingly, in her own creative adaptation, Alice showed (as a university student) some of the material selection of *both* Lee and Oxford's (2008) high school *and* university students: among the "random things" at hand were secondary sources for class research, class texts themselves, websites, and quite likely, other textual and not-so-textual sources from social media, given her habits and interests. Alice's hedging around how she "kind of" memorizes was telling: while individual expressions may themselves be important as task-based demonstrations of language competence (much as creating real or virtual decks of flashcards can help language learners expand vocabulary), Alice's browsing practices suggested routines and habits consistent with her high level of motivation to learn English comfortably.

Alice further exemplified her broad approach to research in a formal paper, in which her browsing habit and her growing familiarity with newswriting directly informed her technical definition of a psychological disorder. Perceiving some room for creativity within her instructor's requirements, Alice motivated her own writing through personal interest combined with her use of detailed news articles as a storehouse of their own:

A: So uh, for the Abnormal Psychology paper [in a course with the same title], I focused on defining the actual and true meaning of sexual masochism and sadism disorder. . . . Cause if it's going to be called a disorder, it has to have like some characteristics, cause um, not all the sadists, sadistic and masochistic behaviors are disorders. And the textbook defined what it was, shortly. . . . I decided to use news articles, because I thought it was going to be easy for me to use real examples, like incidents that happened, with sexual harassment—

. . . J: Was that uh, how did writing that paper go, what was um, easy, hard, enjoyable, not enjoyable?

A: I chose it because I thought it would be fun, but actually it wasn't because it was harder for me to find like sources, scholarly sources, that was written about that. I mean, there were a lot of sources about that, but not many that I could actually use for the paper.

J: Why's that?

A: I don't remember exactly, but I think it was because it was too specific. And the textbook only defined the meaning, so to match with the textbook, I had to, yeah, I think that's why it was so hard, there wasn't a lot of sources.

J: So you thought it was going to be easy, it was not as easy as you thought it was going to be, how did it turn out? Like, how successful was it?

A: So, at first, I thought it was going to be easy, but then I realized that it wasn't too easy. But when I was using news articles, when I decided to use news articles, it became better. Because my idea was to first talk about the subject, sadists, sadistic disorder. The sadistic disorder, I define it first, and then um, sadistic disorder and sadistic behavior are two different things, and then I thought, what is actual incident that is a disorder? If it's on the news, and the person was caught by the police, that's going to be a disorder.

For Alice, the textbook definitions and descriptions of specific disorders, while technically useful, did not provide enough descriptive range to motivate her writing. While she read her professor's insistence on APA formatting as a clear *formal* requirement, she also detected significant topical and evidentiary affordances beyond that documentation style, and she turned to news articles covering sexual assault to provide compelling heuristic detail. While her easy equation, "if it's in the news, it must be evidence of a disorder," was highly questionable, her strategy responded to the assignment's content flexibility, rehearsed her copious approach to identifying and repurposing diverse source material, and specifically used examples of newswriting—a collection of genres with which she had become familiar through other coursework and which she was motivated to learn to produce herself, owing in part to her already growing proficiency with and interest in social media.

As I related at the start of this chapter, a clear implication of describing students' abilities as "coping" is that faculty members tend to have rigid expectations. In her reflective comments about interactions with faculty members, Alice related her attempts to cultivate relationships that in turn afforded her not only additional opportunities to understand assignment and course expectations more explicitly but also to develop more "natural" language abilities. At the same time, her reflections revealed at least some faculty members' willingness to respond to the complex campus environment and negotiate expectations. During an interview in her third year at the campus, Alice recalled a shift in her approach to reading that suggested a connection between her perception of faculty members' relative flexibility and the campus' small size:

> A: Before, I think, I think writing took more time for me to finish. Cause, I don't think I knew exactly what professors wanted. And, I was focused on understanding all of the materials I had, but I, as time went by, I realized it's not about understanding everything, so I started using some tactics that I could write things faster, and for, to be able to like, satisfy professor's needs, I think.
>
> J: Okay, what kinds of tactics, you talked about tactics?
>
> A: For example, like I told you um, if I was, if it was my first semester in language and culture class [introductory linguistics course], I think I would have tried to understand all the things in the articles.
>
> J: If you had taken it during your first semester, yeah, okay.
>
> A: Yeah, and I would have cried or something, every day. But I knew that the professor didn't want me to do that. I mean, he

would want me to do that, but he knew that it was difficult, and what he mainly wanted was for us to focus on more important things that he taught during classes. Yeah, it's not, not um, it's not. Important things don't mean difficult things. . . .

J: Are there other tactics that you've used? It sounds like the tactic there is that you've learned to read, like if you're looking at really difficult articles, you read them, you choose what to read, you're being selective about what you read, rather than trying to like start at the beginning and go all of the way through?

A: I talk to professors. And I focus on what they say, because I think, if they're giving us what to write, like, assignments, they want something, I think. And I think the most important thing to focus on is to that, what they want. What they want to try to teach us, through the whole classes. Um, yeah, I try to think about that, and then I try to listen to what they say, and I try to talk to them personally, if I can. I could all the time, because it's a small campus here. That was really helpful, for me to understand what they wanted.

Alice's general approach is easy to characterize in terms she, herself, provided: give the professor what s/he wants—an approach that underlies many coping strategies. Beneath that superficial description, though, lies a more complex response rooted in Alice's ongoing language learning and socialization. Granted, even as an introductory course, the language and culture class Alice remembered typically included at least some examples of scholarly literature, which can overwhelm students with jargon and give rise to the kind of survival impulse ("understand all the things in the articles") Alice mentions. That impulse was visible to me on one of the first mornings of my first semester on campus: I walked into my assigned classroom to find the whiteboard covered with math terminology. Since Alice was in the class I was about to meet there, I asked her about all the terms, and she told me several students had been in the room late the night before writing and memorizing vocabulary for their online math course. So in relation to Alice's and other students' likely bleary-eyed attempts to gloss math terms, Alice's habit of regularly meeting faculty members in office hours appeared to be a ploy to determine what they really want. That is, it was a coping strategy.

But the motivations surrounding Alice's interactions with faculty members were nuanced—as were faculty members' own motivations for meeting Alice and other students. While Alice related, for instance, that the instructor for her language and culture course may ideally have wanted her to learn "all the things in the articles," she suggested that his more pragmatic/daily attitude was that "important things don't mean difficult things." It is not clear from Alice's comments whether that phrasing came word for word from her instructor or whether it represented her pithy summary of what she was learning as she developed time/load management strategies through the language and culture course. However, her comment provided evidence of at least implicit negotiation of expectations between student and faculty, and it also pointed to a range of both academic and social rationales for individual meetings. Alice repeated her goal of learning more and more about "what they [faculty members] want," but she also expressed that she consistently tried to listen to them—in class and one on one. So read in a wider context of Alice's desire for more natural English language ability, that emphasis on listening reflected the specific goal of listening for evidence of assignment/course criteria, but it also reflected a broader goal of achieving more comfortable competence.

In addition, Alice's reported interactions with her language and culture instructor, and direct responses from faculty informants in my interviews with them, pointed to faculty members' understanding that their expectations may (need to) be in play. Again, considering international students' agency in writing-intensive courses in terms (solely) of "coping" positions them as learners who need to accede to staid, intransigent, and tacit faculty demands. But faculty informants directly and indirectly signaled that they were aware of the affordances of their relatively insular and culturally/linguistically complex context. Alice readily perceived that her linguistics instructor, for instance, had idealized expectations that were pitched high but that he was willing—at least in response to students who, like Alice, approached him individually—to make such expectations more apparent and approachable. In other comments, Alice expressed her perception that two other faculty members seemed both to comment on the "natural" quality of Alice's writing and to prompt her to office meetings in which they could elaborate on their responses to her:

> J: So those [comments by Professor W] are comments overall about the paper? What are the comments about?
>
> A: Overall about the paper.
>
> J: Okay.
>
> A: And the last comment he gave me was very simple because I don't know about other students actually. Because I drop by his office for every assignment. So I get his feedback verbally, in person.

J: So you get a lot of feedback ahead of time.

A: And it's mostly about my grammatical mistakes. And even when it's not wrong grammatically, it sounds unnatural because I'm not a native speaker. So he tries to correct that. And Professor M, he writes comments on paper. Yeah, on our paper. Like, next to paper, like Word.

J: On Word, so he uses the comment utility in Word to make comments okay.

A: And he comments on yeah, grammatical mistakes. Overall flow. And that's about it. I actually, I also visit his office every time. For every assignment.

J: When he's giving you verbal feedback, I mean, both of them are, is that also about grammar? Sitting down with you and noticing the places

A: Yeah, so main problem I have for my papers is mostly uh, grammatical mistakes. And unnaturally.

J: So unnatural. Is it words that you're using that seem unnatural?

A: Unnatural expressions. Words.

To Alice, Professor W's most recent comments were "simple," plausibly because both he and she were acclimated to frequent individual office visits, during which both could further discuss problems or questions in more detail. But even Professor M, who provided more verbose and interlineal comments, seemed to anticipate and prioritize individual conferences. In an interview Professor M had with me separately, he noted his belief that students at the Asia Campus were "more humble" than the primarily native English-speaking students he had taught at the U.S.-based campus—that the Korea-based students "know that they are speaking in a foreign dialect ... [and] are understanding when you correct them." But that corrective expectation (whether in person or through the learning management system) was inevitably complicated when students such as Alice visited Professor M's office not only after receiving feedback but at early/intermediate stages of assignments. And specifically for Alice, those visits created opportunities to reinforce/clarify corrected errors but also to work that much more on "naturalizing" English expression through conversation.

Cutting Two Ways: Faculty Adaptation and Ambivalence

Additional faculty interviews reveal further details about the context in which "natural" language work can develop, including a shared understanding of advantages and challenges of the small campus, the proximity of faculty members and students, and the comparative effects of new versus returning instructors. While the Asia Campus is self-consciously an English-medium institution *academically*, it is highly multilingual on a social and otherwise day-to-day basis. The mix of an increasingly diverse international student body and faculty, staff, and administrators who speak English and Korean at widely divergent levels of proficiency and comfort—all at a campus embedded in a rapidly growing Korean city—means that faculty encounter cultural and linguistic differences as quickly as they walk out of their offices/apartments, if not before. The amount of English that colleagues and I encountered around the self-consciously international campus and city we occupied was increasing as the product selection in local stores I mentioned in Chapter 2 was westernizing. But campus-wide early morning announcements about heating, air conditioning, and/or other residential services continued mostly in Korean only. That kind of complex daily mixture inevitably informed adaptations in teaching at the Asia Campus, where teaching and other quotidian activities co-occurred in close quarters. Professor W relates that

> one of the biggest things is obviously the language barrier. Because not in terms of, I mean we understand each other fine. I will say that I find myself constantly, and I had no idea I do this as much as I do, that I use like idioms all the time. Sayings. And when I say them I think that they have no idea what I'm saying. Nobody says anything, but then I have to say, do you understand what that was?
>
> J: Great, that was a football metaphor. I gotta walk that back.
>
> W: So that's something that I didn't realize that I do all the time, and I do.

In the same interview, Professor W relates his on-the-spot reflection in the face of student responses to an unexpectedly challenging assignment. In a class focusing on communication law, he had assigned students to present on some *ethical* (not technically *legal*) considerations of free speech. While Professor W had facilitated classroom discussions about the different scope of law versus ethics, he noted that they [the students] were talking about all the things that have legal repercussions. And, and in the, in our assignments, I put you know, everything was coming from this particular chapter, and it was on free speech theories, and so that was clear. But no one came in to me and said, hey, I don't understand what this is about. They just prepared it. And I thought, in the US, if there was this problem, my students would have come to me and said, I'm not sure I understand exactly what you want us to cover.

J: Right.

W: And here they prepared it, and they just did it. And I was sitting there thinking, I've got to change this. I've got to like, require that they come up with an outline and then bring it in to me, and we'll sit down with it and we can go over if it's on the right track or not. And that's not something that I've had to do in the past. But I feel like it's something that I'm going to have to do here. And unfortunately, I'm kind of figuring this out a little, but this that has happened repeatedly, right? Where you figure certain things out a little late in the game. And you're like, that's something that next time I can clearly repair.

Professor W thus responded to students' misunderstanding by doubling down on his felt responsibility to do more to adapt to them. Additionally, he recognized in this 2016 interview that he was just at the start of this stay at the Asia Campus—and in many ways at the start of the life of the campus overall. Again, comparative campus size and the proximity of student and faculty working and living space prompted Professor W to understand that, while he felt a need to adjust his up-front pedagogical strategy to include more formative feedback, he had some built-in structural support for such adjustments.

By 2018, Professor B of the psychology department could detect that the small size and close quarters of both faculty and student cohorts indeed remained a persistent factor, creating a kind of student-faculty ecology that was variously sustained and perturbed. Most significant for her was the mix of students' growing familiarity with continuing faculty members through successive courses and their uncertainty about new faculty. That mix appeared to create an interface at which students' strategies to adjust to writing expectations were thrown into relief:

I think one of the unique aspects of [the Asia Campus] is that students are very in tune to, because they're more likely to take the same faculty across multiple courses, right? That happens of course in [the] home campus as well, but not to the same extent, where you see the same student for two or three years running. So I think students here tend to be slightly more sensitive to newer faculty, because they're not sure what to expect. So even when the course you know, [Psychology] 1010 [an introductory course] versus statistics, they're very different courses, in terms of the content. But I'm sort of the steady factor. So they have some sense of my expectations or standards. Or even like, classroom policies. So when I was first here, there was a lot of at least I picked up on a lot of anxiety about what I was looking for in writing assignments—really any type of assignments, group projects—so I've gotten into the habit of having pretty thorough expectations on Canvas, so I post that under the assignments. So if you have this paper due, I try to describe the skills that they will be practicing, the learning objective, as a broad idea, and then I talk about specific points that I am going to be looking for. Usually, what I am looking for, a couple of different things. One is, and I struggle with this here, students often assume that the audience knows a lot more than what they do. So it's like they're writing to me personally. So they'll introduce a concept or a critical study, and it's just referred to in this broad way. . . . And so, what I am always telling them is, you are writing as a form of communication, and you should imagine this is going out to an unknown audience. You don't know what their background with the material is. Don't write to me.

For Professor B, relatively consistent and tight student-faculty interactions afforded by the Asia Campus' size and by the cohesion of its faculty cut two ways. Students had opportunities to cultivate familiarity with course expectations through continuous contact and through recursion—even if such expectations were not necessarily made explicit. However, that familiarity is easily disturbed by the arrival of new faculty members, who may unwittingly be sources of student anxiety not only in the campus' early stages but in years to come. Realistically, while administrators, the governing Foundation, and other authorities have wanted to attract faculty members to the Asia Campus for long terms, much of the faculty complement has been transitory compared to U.S.-based colleagues. But while students can build steady and productive relationships with persistent faculty, that steadiness can prompt them to write arguments that appeal too personally, reflecting students' sensitivity to faculty members' idiosyncrasies over other disciplinary or broader public readers' needs and expectations.

After students' transition to the U.S.-based campus, their natural language work continues, coupled with their desire to continue building both academic and social capital and the challenges of squaring their academic and personal lives. As much as students and faculty members at the Asia Campus focused on academic preparation to work with other major faculty members and to take advantage of wider-ranging opportunities afforded by the much larger and more established U.S.-based campus, it was also clear that students faced some additional challenges that prompted the university to appoint a recently returned Asia Campus student affairs administrator to oversee students' transitions. At times, the academic and social domains of those transitions can seem to diverge. Another psychology faculty member, Professor E, related as much in a 2018 interview:

> E: I had another Asia campus student in that ["Brain and Behavior"] class, and I think she, she struggled with writing a little bit less, but similar errors in her writing. I was noticing that on one of the exams, she just decided not to do any of the short answer questions, I mean, potentially because of how I structure the exam.
>
> J: Right.
>
> E: So perhaps, making an adaptive decision. One thing, well, she came to office hours one time, and I was struck by the fact that she bowed when she left, I had never had a student do that. And she actually, actually volunteered to work in my lab for a little while. . . . She was working in my lab, and because she had had a grandparent who developed Alzheimer's disease, and she was very interested in the impact it had had on the other spouse, on the other grandparent. She was in my lab, which is an EEG lab, but she's really interested in a social psychological kind of question. So anyway, in the course of talking to her about this, she was kind of somewhat typical of many undergrads, in not really having a sense of the level one needs to get at to be competitive at graduate-level studies, relative to your depth in the field. But also, she was talking to me about

life in Korea as a young woman, and all the pressures that she would be facing—

J: Wow, okay.

E: To be married, and to be at a certain point in her career, and so it was clear that on the one hand, she was very invested in staying in the US and getting into a doc program. But that— you know, in this conversation I think it was very hard for her to hear how much further she needed to get to be competitive for that kind of thing. So you know, so I just sort of empathized with her situation. . . . I think she communicated at one point with me, that she was feeling pretty isolated socially, I think that was, oh yeah, that was one of her motivations for joining my lab. We had talked about her interests, and I was like, I don't really know if my lab is the best thing. And she was like, well, I'm really just looking for a way to meet some other students, and have some more connections.

It is perhaps telling that Professor E characterized this (unnamed) post-transition Asia Campus student's avoidance of written short-response questions on an exam as an "adaptive decision." For this faculty member, the student's still-emerging language/writing proficiency and subject matter knowledge prompted her to respond to a testing situation in a way that maximized her possibility to succeed. Professor E's ambivalent response to the student's strategy extended to the student's volunteer work in his neuropsychology lab. While the student articulated a personal motivation to learn more about Alzheimer's disease, and while her presence and work there were apparently not unwelcome, Professor E remained uncertain about her fit as a function of her disparate interests and her aptitude. However, the student's perseverance seemed to have won over Professor E to some extent. While, as he relates, the student was not taking the strong hint that she would not likely create a successful application for graduate study, Professor E recognized that the student's lab work represented both a deeply felt tie to her Korean family and an equally felt motivation to create social connections on the U.S. campus—evidence, I argue, of ongoing natural language work.

A "Natural" Role?: From Learning to Teaching

This student's strategy to inhabit premium and highly interactive academic space may, to Professor E at least, have promised little academic payoff.

However, in at least one other case, social and academic strategies and goals seem to have aligned much more closely. In a 2018 interview, Alice related that she had petitioned to retake an upper-division grammar and stylistics course. Rather than permitting her to re-enroll, the campus' Chief Academic Officer negotiated the addition of a special topics course to the schedule, permitting Alice to take credited hours and to work as a teaching assistant for a newly activated foundational English language development class. Thus, Alice gained an opportunity for some more language learning—this time combined with teaching experience. The combination seemed to create not only some immediate English reinforcement for Alice but also additional intellectual and social dividends for her and for the non-native English-speaking head instructor.

> A: I teach basic grammar to the students, and yeah, it's, I [also] do weekly reflection, weekly writing reflection assignments, like a page, one page sample reflection about anything that's related to second language learning.
>
> J: Okay, your own second language learning?
>
> A: Mm hmm.
>
> J: Okay.
>
> A: And what else? Oh, actually I gave a 40-minute presentation, like I taught a class like twice.
>
> . . .
>
> J: So who, the reflections that you're writing about being a second language learner, are you writing those in, are you submitted them to [Professor O, the course instructor] or to—
>
> A: To her.
>
> J: To her, okay, so is she responding? Are you guys like writing back and forth?
>
> A: She's not like correcting my grammar, but she would comment, for example, I think the last time, I wrote about how Koreans use some words, English words differently from a native speaker. Like, we would actually use "sexy," like, the word "sexy" in a very like light way. Like, we would have like a hash up, with the name is like "sexy dog."

J: Yeah, sexy dog, we saw that.

A: And that's exactly why, we don't think that like sexy is some like actual sexual word.

J: Right.

A: We think it's like cool or charming, so yeah, I wrote about that and Professor O said, "Oh yeah, I saw that too. It was bizarre, thanks for the information."

Through reflective writing technically assigned in the special topics course (which was effectively a directed/independent study), Alice engaged with Professor O about language acquisition—a topic both were apt to find personally as well as academically relevant. In fact, the response Alice recalled here concerns idiomatic and nonidiomatic uses of the adjective "sexy," various uses of which can cause confusion if not outright embarrassment among diverse English language speakers. Alice and Professor O thus shared similar questions about related "hash ups" as they shared the experience of teaching newly arrived students whose own English proficiency was developing.

Alice also related in more specific terms some of her contributions to course material, including conducting two class meetings and creating related videos. Both activities, it turns out, would prove to be professionally and personally relevant, further exemplifying "natural" connections between academic and nonacademic practices. As I related earlier, Alice had, before and during her enrollment at the Asia Campus, created a series of videos about topics ranging from intercultural communication to living in Canada to food, and she shared them, mostly via YouTube. She maintained at least an occasional online presence on YouTube and through other domestic and international social media. After a post-graduation internship in Spain with the International Olympic Committee, Alice returned to Korea, where she began applying for highly lucrative positions in Korea's white-hot private teaching sector. Perhaps true to her multimodal composition experience, she aspired to become a so-called "star teacher," a TV- and online media-based instructor-entertainer mashup of English tutor and K-pop celebrity. I noticed one morning on Instagram several months ago that she had posted an anime-style pencil drawing of herself with oversized eyes and a high collar and necktie with the caption, "pretty happy about my career decision now." In response to an Instagram direct message, Alice wrote that she was starting work for a large Seoul-based language training provider and that she was "getting lots and lots of brutal criticism" because she had little previous teaching experience before her hire. A couple of months later, I exchanged Instagram messages with

Alice, observing that she had talked a lot with me about wanting to become a more "natural" English speaker and asking whether she thought she had. She responded that she thought so but that friends of hers (whom she had known since they all entered the university in Fall 2014) told her she sounded the same. She went on to write that "people seem to make judgments based on accent unconsciously," a belief that continued to prompt her to emulate natural/native speakers.

Discussion

Writing teaching and learning at the Asia Campus inevitably interanimate with other activities and phenomena at many scales. Writing and language development across both the Asia and U.S. campuses exemplify what Urie Bronfenbrenner (1979), in the context of human development, termed "a system of nested eco-systems" subject to perturbing or ripple effects from one scale/level to another. Thus, students' "coping" is more appropriately understood as a range of actions that account for ecological complexity, and teachers' expectations are more appropriately understood as negotiations within the ecosystems that nest and overlap at the Asia Campus. Additionally, the effects of that complexity extend to student and faculty interactions at the U.S.-based campus, at which traditional linear narratives of students' progress are, again, disrupted by ecological considerations. Across both campuses, students' and faculty members' expectations, anxieties, projections, and responses demonstrate the emergence of "transnational social space" (Faist et al., 2013), in which student-faculty negotiations arose interstitially, influenced by the "export" model of international education that the university had ostensibly established but also responding to local campus and city conditions and exigencies.

To be sure, student participants' language acquisition continued through their time at both campuses, and faculty members noted and attempted to adapt to evidence of that acquisition. But as Leo van Lier (2004) argues, language learning is emergent: it arises from a collection of elements in ways that, even if the elements can be counted, exceed that sum. Using the metaphor of young children learning the game of soccer/football, van Lier notes that basic rules eventually give way to young athletes' development of a "feel for the game" in which "the game reorganizes itself from 'running after the ball wherever it rolls' to 'moving the ball around collaboratively in strategic ways'" (p. 81). Elsewhere, van Lier argues that "teaching does not cause learning" (2004, p. 196) any more than rules "cause" the game. While the "rules" of the "game" remain consistent, the ways players orient themselves certainly evolve as play continues so that knowing the rules however well does not directly translate to effective play. As Christine Pearson Casanave (2002) argues in describing the "language games" of graduate students in her study, the game metaphor, while seeming to be an unserious way to describe the importance of language work in multinational/transnational settings, accurately captures the tenuous balance of rules, boundaries, and creativity inherent to language acquisition. Indeed, Diane Larsen-Freeman (2014) presses on the term "acquisition" itself and argues for a shift in applied linguists' thinking from *acquisition* to language *development* because she understands the former term to be inaccurate. Acquisition for Larsen-Freeman implies that there is a stage at/beyond which a person developing language competencies may "have" the language, while development suggests precisely the kind of emergence "through use in real time," evolution, and synergy that is more typical of ecologies (p. 494; also see Marshall & Marr, 2018; Marshall & Moore, 2013).

If the contexts in which Alice, her peers, and their faculty members/instructors taught, learned, and worked were nested ecosystems, it is perhaps no surprise that "natural" emerged as a way to describe desirable language development. Underlying such development is what Lei (2008), following van Lier (2004), described as an approach to ongoing language learning that "potentially involves the whole world" (Lei, 2008, p. 219). Indeed, it seems clear that some of Alice's, other students', and instructors' work responded to a very wide set of academic, social, and material considerations—though not always consciously. To be sure, students and instructors have strategized within course, curricular, and disciplinary expectations. Alice's memorization-for-extemporaneity approach to composing and delivering a public speaking assignment was strategic, and even resistant. Her academically purposeful research and frequent office visits were clearly also socially inflected opportunities to habituate to what she considered natural expression and interaction. Professor E's unnamed student's maneuvering into a lab for which she had little academic expertise but significant social motivation was also highly purposeful, and it demonstrated the student's knowledge that interactions in the lab were as important to her development as to the lab's explicit function. At the same time, Professor W and Professor B separately related different ways that the complex overlapping context of the Asia Campus prompts actions not necessarily conscious but certainly adaptive. Professor W's teaching and responses have been affected both by students' encounters with his expectations about writing and by his sensitivity to the local linguistic scene—in which he himself was surrounded by unfamiliar language practices. Professor B observed that the small size of the campus and its relatively high staff turnover meant students were apt to create and solidify relationships with faculty when they could—a peculiarity of the Asia Campus compared to its better-established U.S.-based counterpart. For that matter, Alice's work with Professor O, while formally a teaching assistantship and independent study in one, created opportunities for both student and teacher to adapt to and learn from each other in a multilingual context while both of them continued their English-language development.

Reconceptualizing students' coping as a range of "natural" adaptations to a nested ecosystem should prompt wider awareness for teachers, students, and researchers. The "linguistic environment immediately increases in complexity when we envisage a learner physically, socially, and mentally moving around a multidimensional semiotic space" (van Lier, 2004, p. 93). So the shift from seeing "coping" to detecting "natural" language work is a way to recast multi-lingual composers in terms that foreground their agency and also the agency and adaptability of instructors, who are often considered in composition literature in terms as limited as those used for students themselves.

However, given the concentric contexts for this transnational educational experiment, which I outlined earlier, it is important to note that students' agency may lead to outcomes many educators may not prefer or may critically question. In Alice's case, for instance, her experiences in major coursework, as a teaching assistant, as a social media user, and as a media intern led her to an initial career choice as a so-called "star teacher" in Korea. Korea's overheated English education market makes such a choice indeed seem to be a natural one: the most famous teachers in after-hours "cram schools" (called *hagwons* in Korea) and/or on television can earn millions of dollars annually (Fifield, 2014). Thus, Alice's own awareness of Korea's educational ecology prompted her to act in a way responsive to available resources not only within her trans-national campus but within the whole transnational educational and social scene she inhabited. Just as there is no way to disentangle the educational experiment from the nested university, national, and neoliberal/international ecologies, there is no way to disentangle students' and instructors' interactions and reflections from the affordances and constraints that enable and help direct them. That dense connection is a critical lesson for instructors, pro-grams, and campuses as they encounter the limits of advanced international planning.

6

"Well Mixed-Up": Pressures on English Competence, Perceptions, and Identity

In Chapter 1, I discussed Korea's complex and evolving relationship with the English language and specifically with English language teaching and learning. As I described, Korea has invested and continues to invest heavily in English as a nation and at the level of individual families, who at times extend themselves transnationally in bids to maximize educational and other social opportunities. But Korea also demonstrates ambivalence about the sociocultural effects of English learning, English proficiency, and associated social capital. Scholarly literature in applied linguistics and anthropology calls attention not only to the high social stakes of learning English but also to shifting definitions of "competence" in the language. That conflict is certainly present in Korea. As Korea has intensified its efforts to participate in a globalized economy, it has also intensified its investment in English, creating opportunities for teachers, translators, and others who can literally and figuratively capitalize. However, those opportunities can bring pressures different from studying for and passing traditional language tests. High-stakes English testing for school and university entry, course placement, and job interviews remains solidly in place, but Korea's ongoing project of globalization injects uncertainty into what English proficiency means. While relevant scholarship has been developing a vocabulary for English competencies in Korea that is more expansive than the traditional native-nonnative speaker distinction, transnational education—just to name one emerging transnational industry in Korea—is laying an ever more diverse terrain as longstanding patterns of in- and out-migration to and from Korea change.

In this chapter, I focus on the perspectives and experiences of David, one of my student participants, whose history as a fluent bilingual speaker of Korean and English and as a U.S. citizen who had never entered the United States before attending the U.S.-based campus of my university, concisely encapsulates the current complexity of English-language sociolinguistics in Korea and at my own transnational site. David's academic work as well as his reflections on courses, assignments, and interactions with peers and faculty members confirm a number of scholarly claims about Korean perceptions of domestic versus international English learning and about the pressures of English-language achievement among (ethnic and/or national)

Koreans. But David's case also adds nuance to existing understandings of the ways students position themselves as competent English users given the complexities both of his (and my) emerging university context and of his own identity. As David makes sense of his own position relative to peers, instructors, and the university, he implicitly highlights the pressures that Korea's cultural and educational evolution exert on conceptions of transfer, on teaching and learning, and on students' competencies and identities in this transnational experiment.

"Semi-Forced": Conspicuous English Competence Among Peers

As I related in Chapter 1, a high level of competence in English is a cherished commodity in Korea, historically quantified as high standardized test scores. But as Cho (2015, 2017) observes among professional translators, English competence has really evolved to become a function of learners' adeptness at meeting shifting standards that are often implicit. So a *guknaepa* learner's formal facility with English acquired in Korean schools may seem static compared to a *haewaepa* learner's fluid, comfortable—even glamorous—competence acquired from travel and other foreign contacts.[20] Unlike Cho (2015, 2017) and the peers she discusses, David was not a professional translator, but his background, competencies, and interactions at the Asia Campus exemplified some of the same patterns Cho observes among *haewaepa* and *guknaepa* subjects. At the same time, David's identity did not fit neatly into either category—a characteristic that suggests additional contemporary complexity as Korea's self-fashioning as an English-speaking context evolves—in part through my university's transnational experiment.

David started at the Asia Campus in the Fall 2015 semester, and he graduated in Spring 2019 after moving to the U.S.-based campus. While he was born and reared in Korea, he is a citizen of the United States owing to his father's own citizenship, and his father spoke to him exclusively in English while David was growing up. He attended an international school in Korea through his entire 12 years of primary and secondary education before enrolling at the Asia Campus. He had travelled outside Korea to the Philippines on several occasions, but he had never entered the United

---

20   Again, *guknaepa* refers in this context to a Korean national who has largely learned English in domestic Korean schools and other programs, whereas *haewaepa* refers to a Korean national who has encountered English in more varied, typically international settings.

States prior to his enrollment at the U.S.-based campus in Fall 2018. David majored in psychology throughout his enrollment. As I did with other student participants, I met David for relatively extensive semi-structured interviews on annual visits to the Asia Campus in spring 2016, 2017, and 2018. And I met him on an additional occasion in December 2018, near the end of his first semester in the United States. I also collected numerous samples of his writing that included instructor commentary wherever possible, and I opportunistically interviewed professors and instructors he mentioned directly as well as others recommended to me by faculty informants, some of whose comments about their work with Asia Campus students have appeared in other chapters.

Beginning with our first interview in May 2016, I noted, among other topics that began emerging, that my conversations with David turned fairly consistently to group work. In that earliest interview, which focused in part on a general education course on global citizenship all students are required to take, David related a division of group labor in which he believed he occupied the role of English-language expert compared to his peers. A recent change of instructor in the course meant that a faculty member was teaching who was an expert on global public health but who had previously worked exclusively with small groups of graduate students. In some ways, this faculty member's relatively nondirective group-based approach and insistence that students should identify their own topics relevant to global citizenship and urbanism seemed to appeal to David, while positioning him as a highly competent peer:

> Justin[21] W. (JW): You said that you have been sort of volunteered to take the role to be the synthesizer, the editor. And uh, it sort of goes to the person that maybe has the best, or is really fluent in English. How did the group know that you were really good at English? Did they just hear you talk?
>
> David: Um, mostly uh, we did a lot of presentations and peer reviews, so there's that, students know who's good at English, or not.
>
> JW: Through the classes?
>
> D: Through the classes.
>
> JW: Like in your classes, ah, okay, so they just heard you

---

21   Justin traveled with me to the Asia Campus as a graduate research assistant in May 2016.

speaking English. What about the writing, did you ever share your writing with the people, or was it all in talking?

D: Peer reviews, we did peer reviews, and those students who got my writings, they spread the news.

Jay (J): Yeah, cause news travels fast.

JW: Go talk to him, he's got the answers.

D: If you have any problems with writing, just go to him, stuff like that.

David related here a phenomenon similar to the one Cho (2015) noted among professional translators, in which language learners who are similarly highly motivated to continue learning English at a high level, similarly driven by grades/other measures of performance, and similarly keen to identify different levels of competence among themselves quickly spot those who have "got the answers," as Justin mentioned in the interview. And David's observations also resembled Fraiberg et al.'s (2017) depiction of "lords of learning," Chinese students at their U.S. university site who consciously or unwittingly acquire reputations for abilities or study habits that leap quickly between face-to-face classroom interactions and online social platforms (pp. 114–146).

In the small-enrollment, somewhat insular, and still inchoate Asia Campus environment in particular, news of David's own abilities as a "synthesizer" and "editor" certainly would have spread fast, and that familiarity showed in ways that prompted classmates to hail him as a kind of translator with at least some expertise. Again, while educated in English solely in Korea, David attended international schools, and—as some colleagues who have also taught in Korea attest—international school students not only speak and write in English in markedly different ways compared to peers from Korean domestic schools (Jon, 2012, 2013), they also seem to orient more comfortably to the kind of classroom the Asia Campus intended to import from the United States—small, friendly, interactive, participatory (where "participation" typically refers to something like spontaneous speech in critical response to specific questions or invitations to debate). For many students coming from domestic schools where English-medium teaching was in service of distributing "English" as a discrete, commodifiable, acquirable target, the shift from English as a rigorously corrected language act to English as a somewhat more negotiable medium was going to take time. For David, it seemed more familiar both in speaking and in writing. In a first-year writing course "literacy narrative" sample he shared with me, he showed considerable fluency in relating his childhood memory of learning to read English with a school tutor whom he described in the narrative in vivid written detail:

> There stood a tall, white old man (when I said white, I meant white including his hair and beard), wearing like a southern country man. His blue jean and checkered shirt well fitted him along his belt with [a] buffalo mark graved in. . . . He took a book out and told me to sit next to him. The couch was red as if I am supposed to sit on a devil's chair.

In this assignment, which David labeled for me as his first piece of university-level writing, he used such details to exemplify his explicit first-paragraph claim that he used to hate reading books but that "things started to change" as early as first grade, when he met this memorable tutor. As the instructor's written summary comment made clear, David at this early stage after his enrollment met the expectation that he foreground a claim about his own literacy and use engaging narrative detail to back it up. While the instructor noted "a few minor grammar issues," including some marked instances of dropped articles and the potentially mistyped "man" for "hat" in "wearing like a southern country man," David's instructor cast them in his written commentary as problems that could be caught with last-stage proofreading. No doubt, as in the academic/social/professional crossovers that Cho (2015, 2017) and Fraiberg et al. (2017) note, David's early success in and comfort with this common assignment in a U.S.-style writing course would have circulated among peers.

But while David took understandable pride in his (technically imperfect but very fluid) facility with English speech and writing, he also evinced some of the anxiety and even annoyance about that facility sometimes noted in relevant literature. That anxiety emerged in David's comments about how workflow in groups tended to orient around him and how he felt compelled to assume certain tasks because of other group members' relative language proficiency:

> J: How do groups, or the groups that you've worked in, how have you decided who writes what? Does everyone just write a piece of the overall report?

> D: Um, well, uh, for my group, I usually would be the one to merge them all for free, and do all that stuff.

> J: So that's your job you feel like. You're the one that takes what everyone else has written and you put it all together and—

D: Yes. I tell other members to write part of the writing, such as I'll give them kind of assignment or job to do. You write introduction, or you write this topic, you write about this topic, you write conclusion, and stuff like that. But of course, when it comes to me, it's all different as it flows and transition, and all of the stuff, so I need to just fix all of that.

J: So that's what you work on mostly is flow from section to section, or from—

D: And I do write most part as well.

J: Oh, so you do most of the writing as well. Okay, okay, that's interesting. So, I guess a couple of questions about that. What, um, you referred to this really briefly before. But I'm wondering how you got that job. Like, how you got the job of being the one who it seems like you're putting the stuff together, but you're also taking a lot of the lead on writing the document, even though it's a group assignment. How did that happen do you think? Did you volunteer, were you elected?

D: Semi-forced, I would say. I don't know if you've seen other students' paper, but to be honest, they aren't really um, good at grammar and stuff like that. So, somehow I tend to be the better one, so students tend to rely on me grammar wise and punctuations and just fixing and stuff like that as well as to write.

David's references to his "job" in group work are telling indications of his sense of obligation. And so is David's mention of feeling "semi-forced" to lead much of the process and editing of documents/assignments. That language colored David's other comments about being the one to "go to" for writing problems/questions, suggesting that there was indeed a very fine line between his role as a prestigious *haewaepa*-like language model and a role in which he feels pressed into service to coordinate and edit for the sake of his and his classmates' grades. Elsewhere in this interview, the combination of course content, writing demands, and David's own responses to his position among other students came to a fine point: he related that he had heard that students in an earlier iteration of the course wrote much less and that the current course's workload and group work were "complex and intimidating," potentially positioning him even more among classmates as the kind of exotically competent English speaker/writer Cho (2015, 2017) describes among peers in translation courses.

From Hobby to *Haewaepa?*: Expanding Competence and Perspective

As David wrote his way into his major, psychology, he encountered assignments that were at least as complex as his writing for general education courses—writing that was constrained by professional and academic domains in his chosen field—and he continued to exemplify shifting competence and shifting perceptions. In Spring 2017, he was taking the same introductory psychology methods course other student participants have discussed extensively—a course taught by a U.S.-educated faculty member, Professor A, who was herself a Korean national. In the course, David did not consistently or entirely own a position as a local language expert. Indeed, he was clear in subsequent conversations about his sense of English-language writing as an element of psychology that required time to understand. David related that the semester-length IMRAD writing assignment in the methods course was foreign to him from the start:

> For the introduction paper, I got lower grade than I expected. There were more critiques. The one major thing that was kind of surprising to me, is that actually, actually, not really. I can't really explain what I get, what I did wrong. I couldn't fix it, because I don't have any knowledge in that specific area, or how to write in the sense that I've never written a research paper in my life, it's my first time, I don't have much knowledge of the materials that I'm writing about. The variables, and all that stuff. And in that sense, I tried my best, but still, as an expert seeing the paper, she tells me that you should include that, exclude that, move this, things around, stuff like that. So I expected those kinds of feedback for my paper.

As other students (and Professor A) also implied, David related that the transition from his introductory general education courses—especially first-year writing—into the methods course was difficult owing to the difference he and other informants perceived between relatively general expository/argumentative writing about topics of free choice on one hand and discipline-specific writing that requires synthesis of existing literature with new findings in a particular professional format on the other.

However, as in his general education courses, David went on to assert expertise and familiarity despite the different challenges in psychology. In our Spring 2017 interview, David revealed his longtime "hobby" of reading psychology research, which he suggested had predisposed him at an earlier age to relevant contextualizing concepts. While David had not traveled at the point he started that hobby, the availability of English-language materials in his Korean household created for David conditions similar to those that *haewaepa* encounter as they build transnational English proficiency.

> J: Are you feeling more—we'd talked about the writing, obviously, which is what we're most interested in, but the writing and the reading are connected very closely. So do you feel, how do you feel about reading research in psychology now, compared to when you started in the major? Do you feel more confident and about the same?

> D: Actually, I've been reading, one of my interests is reading as a hobby is to read research articles. So I started that when I was in middle school.

> J: Really?

> D: Like, reading different articles and stuff like that. So basically, for that, I have nearly no psychology knowledge, so I just read it and, oh, interesting. Stuff like that. Now, since I do know the terms, more terms, and stuff like that, I do see what they mean in the details. So, I think that's a major difference.

Confidence with new psychological concepts and terms may not have been the only familiarity David acquired through his avocational reading in the field. In an extra credit-bearing writing assignment in his abnormal psychology course, David wrote a mock assessment and initial diagnosis of Alan Turing as portrayed by Benedict Cumberbatch in the film *Imitation Game*. The document was separated into discrete sections providing objective and subjective comments about the character's symptoms (of obsessive-compulsive disorder, autism, and other conditions), explicit connections to the *Diagnostic and Statistical Manual of Mental Disorders (DSM-5)*, and APA-formatted references. Given his perfect score on the assignment, and recalling the range of psychology writing assignments that emphasize adherence to APA style and generic expectations, David's pre-and extracurricular reading may have helped his facility with genre.

Indeed, as the reputation of the methods course grew quickly among students, David was primed to expect the course to be hard. And he soon found it to be. But as difficult as the adjustment to writing in the field was proving to be, David was nevertheless apparently able to transfer at least some of what he had acquired on his own from previous reading. As I reported in Chapter 4, other student participants in psychology and communication majors were arguably transferring knowledge and practices from previous education and experience as they adapted to expectations of their chosen fields and of individual faculty members. But that transfer was not occurring in traditionally defined ways. Transfer among these students was less a matter of carrying knowledge/practices from one domain and applying it in another discretely different domain, and more a matter of adapting those previous experiences in creative and often idiosyncratic ways. Learning, according to the socioculturally inclined literature on transfer I discussed, occurs as learners consciously and unconsciously recycle/adapt what they know and do across what Yrjö Engeström et al. (1995) refer to as "intersecting social worlds" (p. 393). As Roozen (2009) argued in the case of his informant, a longstanding practice of Angelica's personal literacy—journaling—became academically and professionally relevant and useful as she persisted through journalism courses. So Angelica developed as a "literate subject" not solely through vertically integrated school subjects/courses but also through interactions of "home" and "school" literate practices (Roozen, 2009, pp. 567–568). Similarly, David's early habit of reading research articles was, for him, a sticky enough practice that it gave him some generic framing for the new concepts in the methods course.

But the effects of David's experiences, background, and prior education arguably extended beyond his generic familiarity with research-based texts in psychology. David's reflections about his status among peers and about his interactions with faculty members/support staff at both campuses suggested broader, ecological, and affective connections and investments similar to those that emerge in the transnational sites and studies I reviewed in Chapter 1. And those connections may have worked synergistically to affect David's work, the transfer of his knowledge and practices, and his perceptions of himself, peers, and the emerging transnational context. In the same interview in which David discussed the difficulty of writing his psychology paper's introduction, he also related the challenges of other sections of the research article assignment. In doing so, he revealed complexities in his identification with peers:

> In the case of the methods section, there wasn't much of, a lot of interaction or feedback going on, so in that sense, I think that students will have a hard time, difficulties, in writing the methods section. Cause they're new. If they want to know how to write the methods section, they probably have to Google it, or visit the writing center, or something like that.

. . .

> [on literature reviews] Well, if you procrastinate . . . you're pretty much doomed, and a lot of students do, so they expect sort of two days or three days, where actually, they have a month to write. So, if they do that, it's going to be really bad. For me, the hardest part was to identify as many articles related to my topic, and reading those articles, trying to get all this information, because I'm new to them. . . . I think you can never have enough, so by the time I ended my introduction paper, I think I had like 30 references, something like that. Other students had maybe like ten references.

Unlike his discussion of the introduction section, in which he exclusively referred to himself and his own difficulties, David here represented what he takes to be the challenges *other students* will likely have with their relative unfamiliarity with the methods section—novelty that would require their seeking support outside the course and instructor. David went on in comments about literature reviews to focus on his peers somewhat more critically, ascribing to them a tendency to procrastinate, which in turn caused them to collect far fewer sources than seems appropriate. In contrast, David renewed some of his concern about this material's being new to him but expressed confidence at the same time that he had more than enough sources from which to work—that the nature of his challenge was managing the information he had dutifully collected rather than putting off the assignment altogether. Taken together, his perception of his competence and that of his peers revealed interanimations of transfer, teaching and learning, and his and peers' competencies and identities.

Even though David balanced his sense of competence against the challenges of research-based writing in psychology, he was feeling comfortable enough with his emerging subject matter knowledge to think about graduate school. And more immediately, he was continuing to connect his writing and more general language competence both to his peers and to his own complex linguistic and educational background. At this point in his career, he was also connecting his experiences more explicitly to the faculty, academic support, and transnational institution more broadly and critically. Echoing Professor A's concerns about faculty coordination around writing, which I cited in Chapter 4, David made some critical comments in our May 2017 interview about the campus writing center's small capacity and lack of expert support for writing in psychology. But he reserved even sharper critical comments for what he perceived to be the university's differential treatment of students. As he did so—here in a spring 2018 interview—he again distinguished himself from peers in terms of competence and nationality:

> One thing I kind of have been suspicious about this is while I take these courses throughout the semesters, is I feel like they [faculty members] are treating these students as if they're not an American institution. And this is an American institution—they're publicly announcing that. But the professors didn't quite seem like they're treating the students as if they're studying in an American institution. For instance, if we write the same paper on the same topic, and I'm an American, and the other student is a Korean, feels like the professor gives a slight advantage to the Korean students, over the foreign students. . . . I'm usually the one that's peer reviewing other students' papers. So I grade them, I help them, I provide feedback, I proofread their papers and all that stuff. And I'm not a professional, but I can say I'm quite better than the other students here.

Facing his summer 2018 transition to the U.S.-based campus, David here put his explicitly stated identity as an American in play with his emerging familiarity with his field and with his progress as a student in an institution still coming to terms with how best to respond to linguistic and cultural juxtapositions. This is an "American" university invited and financed to operate in English in Korea. And Korean students and their parents are attracted to enrolling there because it is a well-regarded U.S.-based university, but one that nevertheless locates itself no farther away than a few hours' train ride or drive from students' homes. While the U.S.-based campus regards many enrollees at the Asia Campus as "international" students, they are in large part "domestic" students at the Asia Campus. David might well have felt more "international" at the U.S.-based campus than Korean citizens who have already studied there, but he claimed U.S. national identity and some measure of internationalized English competence. On the basis of that competence, David strongly implied that his labor in assisting peers' writing development and even language acquisition was undervalued, and he implied that some of the ways faculty members were attempting to accommodate students (as I also reported in Chapters 4 and 5) may have seemed to David like laxity, if not discrimination.

"American" and "Korean" Across Campuses

After his transition to the US for his final semester of study in 2018, and at the end of his first full semester of coursework there (late fall 2018), David seemed to complicate his assessment of faculty responses to students, pointing to even further nuance about his experiences in and perceptions of the transnational university. While his pre-transition comments quoted above focused on different treatment of "American" (seeming) students, such as himself, and "Korean" students by faculty members at the Asia Campus, his post-transition comments suggested a clear difference *between* the Asia Campus and U.S.-based campus:

> J: What else about how do you think the transition from the Asia Campus to this campus has gone? And you can get into that if it's with regards specifically to, you know, working in a pretty writing intensive major or more broadly about the experience. Because those two might relate, you know?
>
> D: I heard from other students as well as my experience as well, is that Asian campus instructors, professors, strict, work harder than the main campus professors. And this also for the psychology classes as well as the other classes, I heard less stress management as well as just general other classes where professors are strict less, less hard than the Asian campus. And I do believe so, because especially for these two classes [his final courses in the major], the professor was very kind in terms of my gradings, and all that stuff. So that's what really caught me, because I expected them to be—the main campus professors would be much harder in their gradings. Much more professional for some reason. That I wasn't ready for this.
>
> J: How do you mean professional?
>
> D: Well, the main campus professors were . . . more calm and easy going whereas Asian campus professors, they're really strict, they're on the appointment, they follow the rules, they really have to, stuff like that. That was kind of interesting.

The novelty of the Asia Campus and its role in providing general education and foundational major coursework to students who then go to the larger and much more established U.S.-based campus imply, as David suggests, more pressure on Asia Campus faculty members to be strict in managing

coursework and relationships with students—pressure perhaps best exemplified by Professor A's reputation among students as well as by her interview
comments reported in Chapter 4. So David seemed primed to expect that the
strictness he encountered would carry over to the US. And he also seemed
primed to expect that such strictness was synonymous with professionaliza-
tion, in contrast to psychology literature and in contrast to the priorities of
other faculty members I reported in Chapter 4.

David's self-awareness and self-fashioning as a kind of *haewaepa*—a
transnational English speaker—is also relevant to his perceptions of the two
campuses. The differences David attributed to himself and *guknaepa* classmates cut two ways. Other students saw David as a highly proficient English
user on whom they could rely for close language work in high-stakes assignments. David saw himself in explicit terms as someone whose proficiency
and experience gave him a comparative advantage among students—but one
that imposed additional work and responsibility. In implicit terms, David's
status, perceptions, and experiences may have positioned him to be especially sensitive to the cultural and linguistic dynamics of both campuses of
the transnational university, including complex faculty responses to diverse
students. Indeed, it is possible to reconcile the apparent contradiction in his
comments about the comparative rigor of the campuses by recognizing the
fluid nature of his national/cultural/linguistic identity. At the Asia Campus,
David relied on previous familial, educational, and travel experiences to identify as an "American," which gave him a lens through which to view potentially different expectations between himself and "Korean" students. At the
U.S.-based campus, David's identity as a Korean student just arrived from
the Asia Campus gave him a lens through which to view culturally inflected
differences between the campuses. In effect, David was transferring not only
his knowledge and practices, but also his perceptions of this still-inchoate
transnational university. His ambiguous position as a domestically educated
student with *haewaepa* sensibilities as well as a somewhat reluctant "lord of
learning" leveraging past experiences to build and assert competence personalized and concretized the ecologies of language development characterizing
such a transnational scene.

Discussion

In such a complex transnational arrangement, and for a student like David,
terms such as *guknaepa* and *haewaepa* are initially helpful to account for
Korean English users' identities, but they quickly meet a limit as heuristics for mapping language proficiency and educational trajectories onto

"domestic" versus "foreign/well-travelled" categories. Similarly, the "learning quadric" meme Fraiberg et al. (2017, pp. 123–124) identify, on which students locate themselves and others along continua from low to high achievement and low to high effort, does not explain David's situation fully. They argue that the labels "learning lords" and "scumbags," circulated among Chinese students through their dense online social networks, provide a limited and limiting typology for student identities even as students cross national boundaries. Asia Campus students certainly used social media to communicate, study, and pursue leisure, but it is likely that the far less dense and still-inchoate social environment of the campus coupled with its public identity as a U.S. campus in Korea precluded at least some of the academic cliquishness Fraiberg et al. (2017) observed. And David himself, through interviews and writing assignments, resisted settling firmly on anything like a label. In a very personal reading response assignment for his cross-cultural psychology course, David related frustration with the comparative scholarship he was encountering:

> Since people nowadays have been influenced by several different cultures, their thinking process has probably been affected. . . . As myself being a multicultural and bilingual and raised in two different environments, American institution and Korean homeland, I have two cultural perspectives well-mixed up. When we have done an activity in class about different views toward different images, some images I have Korean perspective and other, American perspective.

David was "domestic" in the sense that he grew up in Korea, traveling out of the country only for short periods. He was phenotypically "Korean" to classmates and faculty members but quickly distinguishable because of his comfort with English—an effect of both his international school-based education and the multilingualism of his home, which included his U.S.-born father. He was a high-performing student who, as a psychology major, encountered pragmatic, collaborative expectations about writing and editing similar to those that other student participants encountered—expectations that ran somewhat counter to the individual-focused, appointment-driven pedagogy that he saw to be common at the Asia Campus. Arguably, he was sensitive to the way his phenotypical identity was perceived as he crossed borders to arrive at the U.S.-based campus, where the Asia Campus is an increasingly noteworthy part of an overall strategy of attracting "international" students.

As David related his experience, the novelty and, perhaps, exoticism attaching to him and his proficiency may have translated to "*haewaepa*"-style higher academic expectations for him among both peers and faculty members at the Asia Campus. And his "Korean" identity at the U.S.-based campus may have prompted faculty members there in David's estimation to apply less strict standards in the service of helping him and other "international" students transition. But the various peer and faculty responses to David's representation of language diversity—and his perceptions of them—are not surprising. The university, after all, is a transnational one in which both the "distribution" and "spread" (as Henry Widdowson [1997] would have it) of English as the major language of instruction are occurring, regardless of the country in which a given campus is operating. At the U.S.-based campus, university-level presidential initiatives to increase international enrollments to approach those of peer/aspirational institutions are attracting students not only to historically popular majors in engineering and business but increasingly to majors in the arts, humanities, and social sciences. Economic and social mobility in countries such as Kazakhstan and Vietnam are further diversifying international populations on campus, thus diversifying varieties of/practices with English speaking and writing. Those trends combine with opportunities and pressures of grant writing and other academic/professional publications in ways that can enlist even undergraduate students: as psychology students related in Chapter 4, and as other WID-related research has discussed, generalized textbook correctness in WID contexts often plays a secondary role to field-specific conventions and to getting things done as collaboratively and efficiently as possible. So the traditionally fixed assessments of English competence that Cho (2015, 2017), Lo and Kim (2012), and Park (2012) believe to be obsolescing in Korea are obsolescing more globally as well. In short, preparing students to shift to the U.S. campus may have far less to do with ensuring technically correct English expression and more to do with flexible strategies of adaptation.

But emphasizing and teaching such adaptive strategies will likely compete with the pressures on the Asia Campus, since it is not only a campus of a U.S.-based university but also a visible element of Korea's significant investment in internationalization and "soft power." The educational hub of which the Asia Campus is part represents *both* an opening to international trade, education, migration, and competition *and* a desire to reaffirm and project Korean national identity and pride. To the extent that pride trades off with still-prevalent beliefs about "bad" Korean English proficiency, anxiety among students and at least some faculty members and administrators about producing "competent" English speakers/writers will persist. And students like David will continue to model English's constant and complex "spread" while they also contend with the ongoing pressures of its "distribution."

7 Conclusions

Transnational teaching, learning, administration, and scholarship—including this study—are inflected by both broad and quotidian considerations of being—the "whole world" that Lei (2008, p. 219) attempted to net as the possible range of influences on language development (also see Larsen-Freeman, 2014). So as much as both my university and the nation of Korea (through various expressions in its Ministry of Education, the Incheon Free Economic Zone Authority, and the Incheon Global Campus Foundation) may have imagined a smooth and straightforward experiment in transnational education, the Asia Campus' establishment and early development instead bring to relief some rich, rough terrain—the "terroir" that Chris Thaiss (2012) invokes metaphorically with reference to international writing programs' "geographic, cultural, and personal histories and ambitions" (p. 6). In my study, I am only hinting at that fecundity by focusing on a small group of students and faculty members and a limited and, at times, uneven data set. Since the university—and the Asia Campus in particular—has continued to evolve, my conclusions are also necessarily limited: enrollments are growing; new Asia Campus majors are being added; faculty, staff, and administration are changing; and the entire global enterprise of international and transnational education has been disrupted by a pandemic whose effects will likely last years.

But that global enterprise will continue, pressuring scholars, teachers, and program administrators to balance neat institutional directives against the lived realities that studies like mine have detailed. Even if transnational setups such as mine may not make sense for some other institutions given the challenges and risks of branch/extended campuses I noted in Chapter 1, working across borders in many forms will continue to compel colleges and universities, and such work will continue to require close coordination; communication; tolerance of unpredictability; awareness of different (and potentially divergent) educational, administrative, and even national values and goals; and adaptation. Given such needs, there is clear value in the situatedness and focus of a study such as this one: against a curricular and institutional backdrop of writing "in" courses and "in" disciplines in a transnational educational institution, students and instructors consistently interact, position, negotiate, and evolve, enmeshed in networks that are certainly academic and proto-professional but also political, economic, spatial, and physical/material. Administrators and researchers are enmeshed in many of the same networks, especially to the extent they themselves may also be teaching as well as orienting to new places, new people, and new policies and processes.

As I have observed, documented, analyzed, and directly experienced these complexities, I have approached the goal I articulated in my introduction—to understand what happens to writing as a highly privileged academic activity in a dynamic transnational context. And I have learned much about a very specific "whole world" (Lei, 2008, p. 219) of affordances for and constraints on writing and other literate activities. Of course, those affordances and constraints always surround learning, but they have revealed themselves in especially sharp relief in this study in ways that are relevant to teaching and learning, administration, and ongoing research. In this final chapter, I discuss some concluding observations about and implications for teaching and learning, and also about the activities and considerations that not only surround the transnational academic enterprise but are inextricably bound with it.

Complexities of Teaching for Transnational (Disciplinary) Transfer

The idea that teachers should focus at least as much on multilingual students' experiences and abilities as they do on their academic and language learning needs is not new; however, many institutions and writing programs continue to address students from diverse language backgrounds solely in terms of pedagogical support, if not remediation. As I reviewed in Chapter 5, even the more progressive scholarly efforts to understand students' creative "coping" strategies, for instance, tend to position students as needy language workers—and their instructors and professors as staid and intransigent targets. But the diverse backgrounds, experiences, and negotiations of even the small number of students and faculty members at the Asia Campus highlight a range of alternatives. Students there arrive from domestic Korean high schools and from in-country and foreign international schools, and many have traveled for brief or more extended periods outside Korea. Some, such as David and John, may have at least as much comfort with English as they have with Korean, and they may not necessarily identify primarily as "Korean" in the first place. Others, such as Alice, may be motivated by academic language goals but also by goals of acquiring English for broader social purposes. At the same time, faculty members, all motivated by and eager for the opportunity to teach transnationally, will adapt differently depending on prior experience, ongoing adjustments to the location and the student population, and investment in disciplinary goals. That is, faculty members and students alike will "transfer" knowledge and practices from prior/overlapping literacies into their transnational contacts, and the students will also "transfer" knowledge and practices into subsequent academic, professional, and social literacies.

But as I have noted previously, *transfer*, while a term that circulates widely in WAC/WID, will remain imprecise as a way to describe the development of this sort of complex transnational literate community. Students—and faculty—in my study act as ongoing experimenters, repurposing what the scholars of transfer refer to as "boundary objects"—information or practices durable enough to be carried from one literate context to another but malleable enough to be adapted, often for unpredictable purposes (see, e.g., Roozen, 2009; Wardle & Roozen, 2012; Yancey et al., 2014). David's recall of generic features of psychology articles he read as a hobby, Alice's comfort with the informal language of popular media and her attempts to make her English seem more "natural," Professor W's conversion of classroom space to a "newsroom," and Professor E's use of car traffic patterns to analogize brain structures are all reuses/reapplications of previous knowledge/practices. But even where adaptations are not necessarily positive—such as the potential overreliance Professor B noted among students who were perhaps becoming too comfortable with the small enrollment and their closeness to faculty members—they are nevertheless evidence of teaching and learning that is predictable in its unpredictability. So, as Jwa (2019) argues, students' "educated guesses" about what writing and other literate activity can do in the *next* context require teachers and researchers to focus less on discrete skills or concepts and more on the *ways of transfer*. Alice employed a range of strategies to make her English more "natural," and that goal likely positioned her as a particularly effective teaching assistant for Professor O and as a potential "star teacher" herself. Professor W revised his pedagogy to use the constraints of the Asia Campus as a way to emulate the professional environment of a newsroom. Attending to the "ways of transfer" in this context means attending to creative adaptation to a transnational scene marked by culture and language differences, media saturation, and even the material affordances of built environments (cf. DePalma & Ringer, 2011).

Of course, disciplinarity itself is part of the diversity of such a transnational educational institution, and it is an explicit focus of this study. While faculty participants demonstrated their embeddedness in and their sensitivity to the complexities of their transnational work, they certainly remained intent on the goal of facilitating students' professional literacies. But the specific meanings of "disciplinarity" varied, pressured in part by differing perceptions about the roles language correctness plays in disciplinary competence. As I have related, anxieties in Korea about "correct" and "natural" English inflect the experiences and observations of several of my participants. For instance, on one hand, David's positive experience writing in the already familiar genre of a literacy narrative in his own first-year writing course reinforced what he had learned before coming to campus, and it arguably gave him confidence about his own abilities as he encountered complex expectations in his major and across campuses of the transnational university. On the other hand, David and Professor A both expressed some impatience with what they perceived to be a gap between general writing instruction/support and the specific supports students seemed to need in writing-intensive disciplinary courses, such as the psychology research class. That is, Korean teachers and students who may have felt anxious to demonstrate a high level of English proficiency believed errors in language and formatting needed to be addressed as early and as insistently as possible. While Alice, David, and Jane did perform well academically throughout their careers at both campuses, they might have benefited from more of the two-campus perspective Professors M and W had: arguably, those faculty members' experience at both campuses allowed them to contextualize linguistic and generic concerns within the broader transnational university. And as David particularly experienced after his own transition, faculty at the U.S. campus demonstrated flexibility—an observation that suggests a more complex major/disciplinary target than some Asia Campus students and faculty members anticipated.

Foundational awareness of transfer's—and more broadly literacy's—particular complexity in transnational settings is vital to curricular and course planning, including close articulation from introductory to more advanced courses. The small number of sustainable majors at a branch/extended campus such as this one creates a structural opportunity for more coherent WAC/WID than is usually possible at larger and less centralized campuses. However, a transnational university's extension across space (and time zones) poses a clear challenge for academic departments' cohesive identities. Developing students as emerging academics/professionals who "think like" journalists or psychologists or members of other fields is no doubt a common and important goal, but it is one that requires especially careful coordination where students, faculty, facilities, and other resources are usually widely dispersed. Scheduling and budget constraints may mean different departments stretched across multiple campuses must plan for faculty travel/exchanges individually and inconsistently; however, such movement is an important investment because it affords direct experience with diverse students and with instructors/faculty members who may not ordinarily see one another even though they are formally members of the same department. And as I have related with respect to the dense interconnections among teaching, learning, and the everyday social and material considerations of the Asia Campus, that movement is also important as a way to help faculty members experience, compare, and contrast local conditions.

Cultivating *Terroir* for Transnational WAC/WID

The potential benefit of more cross-campus perspectives on writing as a key university literacy activity hints at the value of a transnational administrative effort to recruit and develop writing-focused faculty colleagues from disparate departments and across an ocean. Even on a single, cohesive campus, WAC/WID scholars consistently observe that faculty members' investments in reflective writing instruction vary drastically: faculty in many disciplines, including those I have briefly surveyed in this study, believe broadly in the importance of writing but often lack professional incentive and/or training to spend time teaching it directly. Writing programs/departments have considerable professional incentive to focus on writing pedagogy. But they may not have staff or resources to lend to fuller WAC/WID coordination or, if they do, they may not want to risk retrenching ideas that writing faculty exist to serve other disciplines. Indeed, the early experience I related in Chapter 2 of advising faculty colleagues across the curriculum to coordinate among themselves and with writing instructors reflects patterns of miscommunication familiar in WAC/WID. While initial faculty colleagues (with one exception) did not express a need for such coordination, Psychology Professor A certainly suggested a need for more cross-communication as the student population grew and as more writing-intensive courses were scheduled.

Apart from professional divisions of labor and the uncertainty that can result from a curriculum-in-progress, all faculty members in the kind of transnational institution my study features confront location-related challenges: if they are working at the "home" campus, for instance, they may be distant enough in space and in real time that connections with faculty colleagues at the branch/extended campus may seem tenuous at best. Relationships they otherwise could have developed with promising students for undergraduate research or for professional mentoring/networking may not form before those students transition—which may not happen until late in the students' majors. Meanwhile, faculty at the branch/extended campus face their own professional and personal challenges. For example, while it was highly unusual for me, a tenured professor, to be working at the Asia Campus, my presence made sense given my research interests and given that I was not under the same kind of publication timeline pressures junior colleagues often must negotiate. Nor was I expected to teach as much as colleagues who were permanently assigned to the Asia Campus. I was privileged that my partner and son could travel to visit me several times during my year there. But the combination of space constraints, inchoate city resources, and lack of primary and secondary education options would have made it highly impractical for them to move to Korea with me full time. Even now, these sorts of constraints mean applicant pools for faculty members at the Asia Campus can tend to be limited to very early-career professionals unattached to families, late-career professionals with personal interest in international teaching and travel, or a small number who have personal ties to Korea. Differences in faculty status between campuses, challenges of maintaining departmental identities trans-nationally, and personal and familial complexities can lead to faculty turn-over—a clear administrative challenge, and one that can pose particular problems for efforts to develop cohesive WAC/WID approaches.

Such programmatic, departmental, and institutional complexities interanimate with many others within the nested ecosystems that constitute transnational campuses such as this one. While scholars including Chris Anson and Christiane Donahue (2015), Donahue (2009), and Martins (2015) specifically examine differences in writing teaching, research, and administration across very different and otherwise unrelated institutions in different countries, their notes of caution are also appropriate within a single "extended" transnational institution. Anson and Donahue (2015), for example, critique monocultural perspectives on writing administration by metaphorically relating travelers' tendencies to think of all agricultural activities as "farming" in terms with which they may already be familiar. But not all arable lands and crops, the authors go on to note, are cultivated or managed the same way. With the equally grounded metaphor, *terroir*, Thaiss (2012) suggests the specificity, locality, and fecundity of local conditions that may be somewhat predictable from afar but that ultimately require close attention and cultivation. In less metaphorical terms, *terroir* translates to students' cultural, linguistic, and educational differences compared to the students with whom many faculty (especially those from another campus of a transnational university) may already have long become familiar. It also translates to the often unexpected and superficially invisible differences *within* a "diverse" student body owing to the co-evolution of a host country and of privileged English language practices. It also means ripple effects of staffing and administrative turnover, faculty visits, the appearance of new courses/ degree programs, changing relationships with other universities sharing space and resources, and communicative and structural challenges between national educational bureaucracies. For me, it invokes the experiment within an experiment within an experiment that has been the site of my study—the extended campus of a major U.S. university that operates on a larger multinational campus in a still-new city while all of that is still under construction.

Transnational WAC/WID and a Whole World

Any scholar-teacher who is involved with transnational WAC/WID efforts will be an attractive candidate for administering those efforts as well. So the lines among scholarship, teaching, and administration that are already blurry in the field may be even more blurry at sites such as mine. As this theoretically informed grounded study demonstrates, continuous empirical sensitivity is vital. While I believe this study has benefited from my approach, I am well aware that this kind of research takes a significant amount of time. And time is rarely a friend to scholars who either lack the resources to conduct such research or who may have the means but also have the pressures of consistent, quantifiable scholarly production. I was fortunate to attract support for travel from willing partners on both campuses; to receive ready and able assistance from eager undergraduate and graduate students; and to carve time to think, analyze, write, and revise from and around other responsibilities. Even in my own privileged position, I cannot always count on that combination.

But I believe scholars, teachers, and administrators working in transnational institutions can and should cultivate their own sensitivities to writing and to writing's surrounds—whether they are conducting formal research or not. Many of them may have been recruited/relocated as part of universities' efforts to promote sameness across transnational space—the unidirectional and isomorphic "smoothness" Wilkins and Huisman (2012) critique. But such plans made "on spec" encounter on-the-ground realities: many of the usual complexities of educational experiences can easily be magnified as the emerging transnational ecology in which students, faculty, staff, administrators, and other community members interact takes shape. And writing as a common and highly privileged academic activity will record, represent, and refract such an ecology.

In fact, writing scholars, teachers, and administrators working in institutions that are not as explicitly extended across space as my own should cultivate similar sensitivities. It can be easy for college and university recruiters, administrators, and even scholar-teacher colleagues at U.S.-based institutions to assume that international and multilingual students' diverse experiences, abilities, and instances of transfer level out "on the ground" through straightforward processes of acclimation. But this study and others demonstrate that language learning is rarely if ever linear, that transfer is complex and even idiosyncratic, that histories and trajectories are always relevant even if they are not immediately available for reflection, and that writing can trace the daily, lived experiences of all of us working in internationalist institutions whether relating those experiences was explicitly part of a writing task or not.

As college and university mission statements continue to trumpet international goals—perhaps in new ways in the wake of a pandemic and of geopolitical instability—transnational, quotidian, messy realities will emerge.

Participants in my study and I could not help but co-build and inhabit a "whole world" (Lei, 2008) of affordances for and constraints on literacies that always surround acquisition and learning. For us, the surrounds in which we and our students were working and living were especially sensible as we inhabited a startup within a startup within a startup. But wherever the *terroir* on which writing and other literate activities occur among those of us who have transnational ties, there is tremendous value in research, teaching, learning, and administration that recognize the co-embeddedness of curriculum, nation, disciplinarity, intercultural anxiety, educational ambitions, identity—the list could easily go on, exemplifying the ways transnational experiments are both very wide ranging and very much grounded.

§ References

Anson, C. M. & Donahue, C. (2015). Deconstructing "writing program administration" in an international context. In D. S. Martins (Ed.), *Transnational writing program administration* (pp. 21–47). Utah State University Press.

Arbes, R. & Bethea, C. (2014, September 27). Songdo, South Korea: City of the future? *The Atlantic*. https://www.theatlantic.com/international/archive/2014/09 /songdo-south-korea-the-city-of-the-future/380849/.

Beaufort, A. (2007). *College writing and beyond: A new framework for university writing instruction*. Utah State University Press.

Bizzell, P. (2017). Who owns English in South Korea? In B. Horner & L. Tetrault (Eds.), *Crossing divides: Exploring translingual writing pedagogies and programs* (pp. 70–86). Utah State University Press.

Blom, R. & Davenport, L. D. (2012). Searching for the core of journalism education: Program directors disagree on curriculum priorities. *Journalism & Mass Communication Educator, 67*(1), 70–86.

Blumer, H. (1954). What is wrong with social theory? *American Sociological Review, 19*(1), 3–10.

Boice, R. (1990). Faculty resistance to writing-intensive courses. *Teaching of Psychology, 17*(1), 13–17.

Bowen, G. A. (2006). Grounded theory and sensitizing concepts. *International Journal of Qualitative Methods, 5*(3), 12–23.

Bronfenbrenner, U. (1979). *The ecology of human development: Experiments by nature and design*. Harvard University Press.

Brooks, R. & Waters, J. (2011). *Student mobilities, migration and the internationalization of higher education*. Springer.

Byean, H. (2015). English, tracking, and neoliberalization of education in South Korea. *TESOL Quarterly, 49*(4), 867–882.

C-BERT. (n.d.). *International campuses*. Retrieved August 1, 2021, from http://cbert .org/resources-data/intl-campus/.

Cai, L. & Hall, C. (2016). Motivations, expectations, and experiences of expatriate academic staff on an international branch campus in China. *Journal of Studies in International Education, 20*(3), 207–222.

Carroll, L. A. (2002). *Rehearsing new roles: How college students develop as writers*. Southern Illinois University Press.

Casanave, C. P. (2002). *Writing games: Multicultural case studies of academic literacy practices in higher education*. Routledge.

Charmaz, K. (2003). Grounded theory: Objectivist and constructivist methods. In N. K. Denzin & Y. S. Lincoln (Eds.), *Strategies for qualitative inquiry* (pp. 249–291). Sage.

Charmaz, K. (2006). *Constructing grounded theory: A practical guide through qualitative analysis*. Sage.

Chiseri-Strater, E. (1991). *Academic literacies: The public and private discourse of university students*. Boynton.

Cho, J. (2015). Sleepless in Seoul: Neoliberalism, English fever, and linguistic insecurity among Korean interpreters. *Multilingua, 34*(5), 687–710.

Cho, J. (2017). *English language ideologies in Korea: Interpreting the past and present*. Springer.

Cicchetti, K. O. (2018). Home away from home? A case study of student transitions to an international branch campus. *Journal of Student Affairs Research and Practice, 55*(4), 452–464.

Collins, S. G. (2005). "Who's this Tong-il?": English, culture and ambivalence in South Korea. *Changing English, 12*(3), 417–429.

Currie, P. (1998). Staying out of trouble: Apparent plagiarism and academic survival. *Journal of Second Language Writing, 7*(1), 1–18.

Demick, B. (2002, March 31). Some in S. Korea opt for a trim when English trips the tongue. *Los Angeles Times*. https://www.latimes.com/archives/la-xpm-2002-mar-31-mn-35590-story.html.

DePalma, M. J. & Ringer, J. M. (2011). Toward a theory of adaptive transfer: Expanding disciplinary discussions of "transfer" in second-language writing and composition studies. *Journal of Second Language Writing, 20*(2), 134–147.

Deuze, M. (2001). Educating "new" journalists: Challenges to the curriculum. *Journalism and Mass Communication Educator, 56*(1), 4–17.

Donahue, C. (2009). "Internationalization" and composition studies: Reorienting the discourse. *College Composition and Communication, 61*(2), 212–243.

Dunn, D. S. (1994). Lessons learned from an interdisciplinary writing course: Implications for student writing in psychology. *Teaching of Psychology, 21*(4), 223–227.

Engeström, Y., Engeström, R. & Kärkkäinen, M. (1995). Polycontextuality and boundary crossing in expert cognition: Learning and problem solving in complex work activities. *Learning and Instruction, 5*(4), 319–336.

Eschenfelder, C. C. (2019). But can they write? Television news industry assessment of the skills of broadcast journalism students and recent graduates. *Journalism and Mass Communication Educator, 74*, 1–7.

Faist, T., Fauser, M. & Reisenauer, E. (2013). *Transnational migration*. John Wiley & Sons.

Fifield, A. (2014, December 30). In education-crazy South Korea, top teachers become multimillionaires. *The Washington Post*. https://www.washingtonpost.com/world/asia_pacific/in-education-crazy-south-korea-top-teachers-become-multimillionaires/2014/12/29/1bf7e7ae-849b-11e4-abcf-5a3d7b3b20b8_story.html.

Fraiberg, S., Wang, X. & You, X. (2017). *Inventing the world grant university: Chinese international students' mobilities, literacies, and identities*. Utah State University Press.

Friedrich, J. (1990). Learning to view psychology as a science: Self-persuasion through writing. *Teaching of Psychology, 17*(1), 23–27.

Glaser, B. G. & Strauss, A. L. (1967). *The discovery of grounded theory: Strategies for qualitative research*. De Gruyter.

Goddard, P. (2003). Implementing and evaluating a writing course for psychology majors. *Teaching of Psychology, 30*(1), 25–29.

Goodman, R. (1986). Education, society and the Korean returnee in anthropological perspective. *Journal of East and West Studies, 15*(2), 35–52.

Haas, C. (1994). Learning to read biology: One student's rhetorical development in college. *Written Communication, 11*(1), 43–84.

Haswell, R. H. (2000). Documenting improvement in college writing: A longitudinal approach. *Written Communication, 17*(3), 307–352.

Herrington, A. J. & Curtis, M. (2000). *Persons in process: Four stories of writing and personal development in college*. National Council of Teachers of English.

Hesford, W. S. & Schell, E. E. (2008). Introduction: Configurations of transnationality: Locating feminist rhetorics. *College English, 70*(5), 461–470.

Hettich, P. (1990). Journal writing: Old fare or nouvelle cuisine? *Teaching of Psychology, 17*(1), 36–39.

Howard, R. M. (1995). Plagiarisms, authorships, and the academic death penalty. *College English, 57*(7), 788–806.

Howard, R. M. (1999). *Standing in the shadow of giants: Plagiarism, authors, collaborators*. Ablex.

Howard, R. M., Serviss, T. & Rodrigue, T. K. (2010). Writing from sources, writing from sentences. *Writing & Pedagogy, 2*(2), 177–192.

Incheon Free Economic Zone. (2018). *IFEZ Incheon Free Economic Zone*. https://www.ifez.go.kr/eng/index.

Incheon Global Campus. (n. d.). *IGC Incheon Global Campus*. Retrieved August 28, 2021, from https://www.igc.or.kr/en/index.do.

Institute of International Education. (2022). *Enrollment Trends*. https://opendoorsdata.org/data/international-students/enrollment-trends/.

Jeon, M. (2009). Globalization and native English speakers in English Programme in Korea (EPIK). *Language, Culture and Curriculum, 22*(3), 231–243.

Jolley, J. M. & Mitchell, M. L. (1990). Two psychologists' experiences with journals. *Teaching of Psychology, 17*(1), 40–41.

Jon, J. E. (2012). Power dynamics with international students: From the perspective of domestic students in Korean higher education. *Higher Education, 64*(4), 441–454.

Jon, J. E. (2013). Realizing internationalization at home in Korean higher education: Promoting domestic students' interaction with international students and intercultural competence. *Journal of Studies in International Education, 17*(4), 455–470.

Jordan, J. (2015). Material translingual ecologies. *College English, 77*(4), 364–382.

Jordan, J. & Jensen, E. (2017). Writing programs, student support, and privatizing international recruitment. In N. DeJoy & B. Smith (Eds.), *Collaborations and innovations: Supporting multilingual writers across campus units* (pp. 39–57). University of Michigan Press.

Jordan, J. & Kedrowicz, A. (2011). Attitudes about graduate L2 writing in engineering: Possibilities for more integrated instruction. *W*, *8*(4). https://doi.org/10.37514/ATD-J.2011.8.4.24.

Jwa, S. (2019). Transfer of knowledge as a mediating tool for learning: Benefits and challenges for ESL writing instruction. *Journal of English for Academic Purposes*, *39*, 109–118.

Kohn Pedersen Fox Associates. (2020). *New Songdo City: Songdo International Business District*. https://www.kpf.com/projects/new-songdo-city.

Lane, J. & Kinser, K. (2013, November 8). *The Asia Pivot in higher education*. C-BERT. http://cbert.org/?blog_post=254.

Larsen-Freeman, D. (2014). Saying what we mean: Making a case for "language acquisition" to become "language development." *Language Teaching*, *48*(4), 491–505.

Lee, J., Han, M. W. & McKerrow, R. E. (2010). English or perish: How contemporary South Korea received, accommodated, and internalized English and American modernity. *Language and Intercultural Communication*, *10*(4), 337–357.

Lee, J. & Kim, H. (2016, April 4). *Coffee wars: South Korea's cafe boom nears saturation point*. Reuters. https://www.reuters.com/article/us-southkorea-coffee-idUSKCN0X12GF.

Lee, K. R. & Oxford, R. (2008). Understanding EFL learners' strategy use and strategy awareness. *Asian EFL Journal*, *10*(1), 7–32.

Leggette, H. R., Redwine, T. & Busick, B. (2020). Through reflective lenses: Enhancing students' perceptions of their media writing skills. *Journalism & Mass Communication Educator*, *75*(1), 81–97.

Lei, X. (2008). Exploring a sociocultural approach to writing strategy research: Mediated actions in writing activities. *Journal of Second Language Writing*, *17*(4), 217–236.

Leki, I. (1995). Coping strategies of ESL students in writing tasks across the curriculum. *TESOL Quarterly*, *29*(2), 235–260.

Leki, I. (2007). *Undergraduates in a second language: Challenges and complexities of academic literacy development*. Routledge.

Levitt, P. & Schiller, N. G. (2004). Conceptualizing simultaneity: A transnational social field perspective on society. *International Migration Review*, *38*(3), 1002–1039. https://doi.org/10.1111/j.1747-7379.2004.tb00227.x.

Lo, A. & Kim, J. C. (2012). Linguistic competency and citizenship: Contrasting portraits of multilingualism in the South Korean popular media. *Journal of Sociolinguistics*, *16*(2), 255–276.

Ludeman, R. B., Osfield, K. J., Hidalgo, E. I., Oste, D. & Wang, H. S. (2009). *Student affairs and services in higher education: Global foundations, issues and best practices*. International Association of Student Affairs and Services (IASAS).

Madigan, R. & Brosamer, J. (1990). Improving the writing skills of students in introductory psychology. *Teaching of Psychology*, *17*(1), 27–30.

Marshall, S. & Marr, J. W. (2018). Teaching multilingual learners in Canadian writing-intensive classrooms: Pedagogy, binaries, and conflicting identities. *Journal of Second Language Writing*, *40*, 32–43.

Marshall, S. & Moore, D. (2013). 2B or not 2B plurilingual? Navigating languages literacies, and plurilingual competence in postsecondary education in Canada. *TESOL Quarterly, 47*(3), 472–499.

Martins, D. S. (Ed.). (2015). *Transnational writing program administration.* Utah State University Press.

Massé, M. H. & Popovich, M. N. (1998). Assessing faculty attitudes toward the teaching of writing. *Journalism & Mass Communication Educator, 53*(3), 50–64.

Miller, R. & Andrews, R. (1993). Robert and Roy's excellent adventure. *WAC Journal, 4*, 109–128. https://doi.org/10.37514/WAC-J.1993.4.1.10.

Mu, C. & Carrington, S. (2007). An investigation of three Chinese students' English writing strategies. *TESL-EJ, 11*(1), 1–23.

Ng, S. W. (2012). Rethinking the mission of internationalization of higher education in the Asia-Pacific region. *Compare: A Journal of Comparative and International Education, 42*(3), 439–459.

Ninnes, P. & Hellstén, M. (2005). Internationalizing higher education: Critical explorations of pedagogy and policy. Springer.

Nordquist, B. (2017). *Literacy and mobility.* Routledge.

Panici, D. A. & McKee, K. B. (1996). Writing-across-the-curriculum within mass communication. *Journalism & Mass Communication Educator, 51*(4), 47–53.

Park, J.-K. (2009). "English fever" in South Korea: Its history and symptoms. *English Today, 25*(1), 50–57.

Park, J. S.-Y. (2012). English as border-crossing: Longing and belonging in the South Korean experience. In V. Rapatahana & P. Bunce (Eds.), *English language as Hydra: Its impacts on non-English language cultures* (pp. 208–220). Multilingual Matters.

Pecorari, D. (2016). Plagiarism, international students, and the second-language writer. In T. Bretag (Ed.), *Handbook of academic integrity* (pp. 537–550). Springer.

Redden, E. (2014, March 12). Amid the branch campus building boom, some universities reject the model. *Inside Higher Ed.* https://www.insidehighered.com/news/2014/03/12/amid-branch-campus-building-boom-some-universities-reject-model.

Redden, E. (2015, March 16). The branch campus boom(s). *Inside Higher Ed.* https://www.insidehighered.com/news/2015/03/16/international-branch-campus-phenomenon-just-fad.

Redden, E. (2019, October 1). Canceled course renews academic freedom concerns. *Inside Higher Ed.* https://www.insidehighered.com/news/2019/10/01/cancellation-course-dissent-yale-nus-campus-singapore-prompted-academic-freedom.

Reid, J. (1998). "Eye" learners and "ear" learners: Identifying the language needs of international student and US resident writers. In P. Byrd & J. M. Reid (Eds.), *Grammar in the composition classroom: Essays on teaching ESL for college-bound students* (pp. 3–17). Heinle.

Roozen, K. (2009). From journals to journalism: Tracing trajectories of literate development. *College Composition and Communication, 60*(3), 541–572.

Shams, F. & Huisman, J. (2016). The role of institutional dual embeddedness in the strategic local adaptation of international branch campuses: Evidence from Malaysia and Singapore. *Studies in Higher Education*, *41*(6), 955–970.

Shi L. (2004). Textual borrowing in second-Language writing. *Written Communication*, *21*(2): 171–200.

Singh, M., Rizvi, F. & Shrestha, M. (2007). Student mobility and the spatial production of cosmopolitan identities. In *Spatial theories of education* (pp. 205–224). Routledge.

Smith, E. J. (1997). Professional and academic levels of a mass media writing course. *Journalism & Mass Communication Educator*, *52*(1), 59–65.

Smoke, T. (1994). Writing as a means of learning. *College ESL*, *4*(2), 1–11.

Spack, R. (1997). The acquisition of academic literacy in a second language: A longitudinal case study. *Written Communication*, *14*(1), 3–62.

Spack, R. (2004). The acquisition of academic literacy in a second language: A longitudinal case study, updated. In V. Zamel & R. Spack (Eds.), *Crossing the curriculum: Multilingual learners in college classrooms* (pp. 19–45). Erlbaum.

Sternglass, M. S. (1993). Writing development as seen through longitudinal research: A case study exemplar. *Written Communication*, *10*(2), 235–261.

Sternglass, M. S. (1997). *Time to know them: A longitudinal study of writing and learning at the college level*. Routledge.

Suk, G.-h. (2015, July 22). 'Konglish' floods into apartment brand names. *The Korea Herald*. http://www.koreaherald.com/view.php?ud=20150722001132.

Thaiss, C. (2012). Origins, aims, and uses of writing programs worldwide: Profiles of academic writing in many places. In C. Thaiss, G. Bräuer, P. Carlino, L. Ganobc-sik-Williams & A. Sinha (Eds.), *Writing programs worldwide: Profiles of academic writing in many places* (pp. 5–22). The WAC Clearinghouse: Parlor Press. https://doi.org/10.37514/PER-B.2012.0346.2.01.

Van Lier, L. (2004). *The ecology and semiotics of language learning: A sociocultural perspective*. Springer.

Vertovec, S. (1999). Conceiving and researching transnationalism. *Ethnic and Racial Studies*, *22*(2), 447–462. https://doi.org/10.1080/014198799329558.

Wardle, E. (2007). Understanding "transfer" from FYC: Preliminary results of a longitudinal study. *WPA*, *31*(1–2), 65–85.

Wardle, E. & Roozen, K. (2012). Addressing the complexity of writing development: Toward an ecological model of assessment. *Assessing Writing*, *17*(2), 106–119.

Wetzel, D. Z. & Reynolds, D. W. (2014). Adaptation across space and time: Revealing pedagogical assumptions. In D. S. Martins (Ed.), *Transnational writing program administration* (pp. 93–116). Utah State University Press.

Widdowson, H. G. (1997). EIL, ESL, EFL: Global issues and local interests. *World Englishes*, *16*(1), 135–146.

Wilkins, S. & Huisman, J. (2012). The international branch campus as transnational strategy in higher education. *Higher Education*, *64*(5), 627–645.

Wolcott, W. (1994). A longitudinal study of six developmental students' performance in reading and writing. *Journal of Basic Writing*, *13*(1), 14–40.

Yancey, K. B., Robertson, L. & Taczak, K. (2014). *Writing across contexts: Transfer, composition, and sites of writing*. Utah State University Press.

Zamel, V. (1995). Strangers in academia: The experiences of faculty and ESL students across the curriculum. *College Composition and Communication, 46*(4), 506–521.

Zehr, D. (1998). Writing in psychology courses. *WAC Journal, 9*, 7–13. https://doi.org/10.37514/WAC-J.1998.9.1.02.

Zehr, D. & Henderson, K. (1994). Buffy, Elvis, and introductory psychology: Two characters in search of a dialogue. *WAC Journal, 5*, 11–22. https://doi.org/10.37514/WAC-J.1994.5.1.02.

§ Appendices

Appendix A: Student Survey, 2015

Please answer each of these questions with as much detail as you can. Since this is an electronic document, **please feel free to add as many lines as you need to answer each question**.

What kinds of schools have you attended, and in which countries? (For example, international schools in Korea or in other countries, only schools in Korea, etc.)

1. For how many years have you studied English in school?

2. How comfortable are you with your English

    In speaking?

    ___ Uncomfortable

    ___ A little comfortable

    ___ Somewhat comfortable

    ___ Comfortable most of the time

    ___ Comfortable all of the time

    In writing?

    ___ Uncomfortable

    ___ A little comfortable

    ___ Somewhat comfortable

    ___ Comfortable most of the time

    ___ Comfortable all of the time

3. What kinds of writing have you done so far in Korean and English? (For example, only academic writing, such as essays, research papers, summaries, etc. Or also personal and/or creative writing, such as stories, poems, Facebook or Naver posts, etc.)

4. What is your major?

5. What kinds of writing do you expect to do in your major? (Be as specific as you can be—for example, news stories, case studies, literature reviews, etc.)

6. What do you do well in writing? What do you feel less confident about?

7. What do professors comment most about in your writing? (For example, thesis statements, level of detail, sentence-level grammar,

organization, spelling, word choice, etc. Try to give very specific examples.)

8. What have you learned about writing since you started as a student at the University of Utah?

9. How has your writing changed since you started as a student at the University of Utah?

Appendix B: Faculty Survey, 2015

Please answer each of these questions with as much detail as you can. Since this is an electronic document, please feel free to add as many lines as you need to answer each question.

10. Which courses do you regularly teach, and in which department(s)/program(s)?

11. What kinds of writing do you assign in your courses? (Please be specific. For example, news or feature articles, summaries, literature reviews, case studies, critical reviews of books or articles, SOAP notes, etc.)

12. When you respond to and/or evaluate student writing, which of the following do you pay particular attention to? (Please mark all that apply.)

____ Appropriateness of student's overall strategy (for instance, the assignment asks for "analysis" and the student responds with analysis)

____ Presence/clarity of "thesis" or main idea(s)

____ Logical argument

____ Level of detail/quality of evidence and examples

____ Audience accommodation (for instance, a "hook" designed to appeal to a reader or compelling quotations/illustrations selected for rhetorical effect)

____ Overall length

____ Organization and flow/cohesion

____ Development of paragraphs and/or sections

____ Sentence-level grammar, including word order and sentence completeness

____ Word choice, including appropriate/correct words and level of formality